Reasons without Rationalism

Reasons without Rationalism

Kieran Setiya

PRINCETON UNIVERSITY PRESS

PRINCETON AND OXFORD

Published by Princeton University Press, 41 William Street,
Princeton, New Jersey 08540
In the United Kingdom: Princeton University Press, 3 Market Place,
Woodstock, Oxfordshire OX20 1SY

Library of Congress Cataloging-in-Publication Data

Setiya, Kieran, 1976–
Reasons without rationalism / Kieran Setiya.
    p.   cm.
Includes bibliographical references and index.
ISBN-13: 978–0-691–12749–1
ISBN-10: 0–691-12749–2
1. Ethics. 2. Virtue. 3. Act (Philosophy). 4. Practical reason. I. Title.
BJ1521.S48 2007
171′.3—dc22   2006010000

British Library Cataloging-in-Publication Data is available

This book has been composed in Sabon

Printed on acid-free paper. ∞

pup.princeton.edu

Printed in the United States of America

10   9   8   7   6   5   4   3   2   1

to *MJG* and *LCM*

CONTENTS

PREFACE

SINCE I WAS ABOUT SIX, I have wanted to write a book. This is not exactly the book that I imagined then—which would have been more strongly influenced by the *Star Wars* trilogy—but it is, at least, a book. I am glad to have managed it.

This would not have been possible without a great deal of help. I would like to thank my parents for their support and for putting up with my decision to become the wrong sort of doctor. Thanks, also, to my brother, for his generosity and good advice, and to my in-laws: Simone, Ed, Susan, and Don.

Although I accept *some* responsibility for the book you are reading, part of the blame must go to my first philosophy teacher, Jeremy Butterfield, for whose encouragement I could not be more grateful. (Without it, I would never have tried to do this for a living.) Many others have helped me by responding to the arguments that follow: Jonathan Beere, Paul Benacerraf, Karin Boxer, Matt Boyle, Michael Bratman, Ruth Chang, John Cooper, John Doris, Anton Ford, Harry Frankfurt, Mark Greenberg, Gil Harman, Benj Hellie, Zena Hitz, Mark Johnston, Doug Lavin, John McDowell, Grant Reaber, Gabriel Richardson, Gideon Rosen, Michael Smith, Jeff Speaks, Sarah Stroud, David Sussman, Michael Thompson, and participants in my fall 2005 seminar on rationality at the University of Pittsburgh. I received valuable comments on some of this material from readers at the *Philosophical Review*, where it appeared as "Explaining Action" (*Philosophical Review* 112 (2003), © Cornell University). It is reprinted here by permission of the publisher. For reading and commenting on the whole manuscript in previous drafts, I am indebted to Gordon Belot, Simon Keller, Jessica Moss, and the anonymous readers for the Press. Throughout this process, Ian Malcolm has been a supportive and insightful editor. Heath Renfroe did a wonderful job of copyediting the text.

Two people deserve special thanks. Much of what I think is right in how I do philosophy, I learned from my friend, Cian Dorr. At least on his part, our conversations have been a model of philosophical dialogue. I feel lucky to know him.

To my wife, Marah Gubar, I cannot express the depth of my love and gratitude. She is my better half and my best friend. If anything in this book speaks truly about what it is to be happy and to live a good life, it is because of her.

Reasons without Rationalism

THIS IS A BOOK about how one should live. And since I take it for granted that what one should do, all things considered, is what there is most reason to do, it is at the same time a book about practical reason. The view it defends is roughly this: that one should live and act as a person of *good character* would live and act, if she were in one's place; one should imitate the ethically virtuous person.

There are complications here. What am I to do when I have managed to end up in a ditch in which no virtuous person could be found? What about the fact that there are many different ways of being good? For the moment, let us set these issues aside.[1] I will argue that we cannot say what it is to have a reason to act, or understand the nature of practical reason, except in terms of ethical virtue. It follows, as I will try to show, that Aristotle was right: we cannot be fully good without the perfection of practical reason, or have that perfection without being good.[2]

When I describe my view to non-philosophers, it is sometimes met with blank incomprehension—not, I think, because its terms are specially obscure, but because it is hard to see why one would bother to defend it. It can seem too obvious a truth to count as a philosophical insight. Of course one *should* act as a virtuous person would. "[There] is no one who needs to be told that he ought to be just and brave and temperate. This is self-evident, and calls for no deliberation" (Pieper 1966: 33). But while I am sympathetic to the spirit of this remark, the claim I am defending is *not* self-evident. What I am arguing is not just that there is a sense of "should" connected with ethical virtue, but that this is the "should" of *practical reason*, of what there is most reason for anyone to do. It is a commonplace of modern moral philosophy that there is at least a nominal distinction here—even for those who hope that practical reason and ethical virtue will converge. My claim is that this distinction, the idea that there are standards of practical reason apart from or independent of good character, is a philosophical mirage.

In saying this, I reject the tradition that descends from Hobbes and Hume to economics and decision theory, on which practical reason is conceived as purely instrumental: it is a matter of means-end efficiency, not of

---

[1] I address the first question in this introduction, and the second in Part Two, section 1.
[2] This is a loose rendering of Aristotle's *Nicomachean Ethics*, 1144b31–2.

ethical virtue.[3] And I reject the Kantian conception of practical reason, on which its standards derive from the nature of agency, as such.[4] On this view, too, the condition of being properly responsive to reasons can be distinguished from the good condition of one's habituated character.

We can see more clearly what is distinctive of my view, and how it conflicts with these traditions, by examining the question "Why should I be moral?" If *ethics* is concerned with how one should live, or what one should do, all things considered, and *ethical virtues* are virtues of character, *morality* can be thought of as *part* of ethics, and the moral virtues as a *subset* of the ethical virtues. It is not, in the end, very easy to say what is distinctive about morality and the moral virtues, if anything. A first thought is that they are essentially *other-regarding*. Thus justice and benevolence are paradigms of moral virtue—by contrast with non-moral virtues like prudence, moderation, and means-end efficiency.[5] Since nothing turns on the significance of grouping the moral virtues together, we need not look for a definition. Instead we can rely directly on our examples. To ask, "Why should I be moral?" is, in effect, to ask, "Why should I be benevolent, or just?"

This question can be heard in two ways. It might express doubts about the standing of justice and benevolence *as* virtues of character—as, for instance, in Nietzsche, on Foot's (2001, ch. 7) account of him, or Callicles in Plato's *Gorgias*. Or it might express doubts about the practical justification of morality that *concede* common assumptions about moral virtue. "Why should I be moral?" is meant to be a question of the second kind: it is asked by someone who is willing to agree that a *virtuous* person would be benevolent and just, in the ordinary sense, but who wants to know what reason he has to follow suit.[6] He accepts that the so-called moral virtues are virtues of character, but wonders why he should not cast them aside.

---

[3] For accounts of this kind, see, especially, Williams (1980; 1989) and Dreier (1997). Williams protests that his view is not instrumentalist, because it has a richer conception of practical thought. But he ties an agent's reasons to his "subjective motivational set," and that is enough to belong to the tradition I have in mind.

[4] For Kantian accounts of practical reason, see Darwall (1983), Gewirth (1978), Korsgaard (1996, 1997), Nagel (1970), and Velleman (1989; 2000b).

[5] A similar distinction is made by Slote (1992: xvi and *passim*). I think it is actually unclear whether means-end efficiency is an unconditional virtue. This issue is discussed in Setiya (2005); see also the conclusion of this book.

[6] As an example of confusion in this area, consider the common mis-reading of Prichard (1912) as being concerned with the relation between practical reason and morality—the second question. In fact, Prichard takes it for granted that obligations provide reasons. His question is about the standing of what we *take* as our obligations *as* genuine obligations. It is thus analogous to the first of the two questions distinguished in the text.

On the view that I defend in this book, his question rests on a mistake. When I say that one should act as a good person acts, I am thinking of good character in general, not the moral virtues in particular. But I treat these virtues—ones like justice and benevolence—in the same way as any others. They are not subordinate to the non-moral virtues of prudence or efficiency, or of "consistency in action."[7] If a virtuous person would be moved by certain considerations, it *follows* that they count as reasons to act. So if justice and benevolence are really virtues, they correspond to reasons in their own right: it belongs to good practical thought to give weight to the kinds of considerations to which the just and benevolent person is sensitive. The answer to the question "Why should I be moral?" is not, on this account, supplied by further *reasons* to be moral, which are certified as reasons by a standard other than ethical virtue. It is supplied by the fact that having the moral virtues is a matter of being responsive to considerations that *therefore* count as reasons to act.

This view contrasts with most of those that figure in recent debate, where it is assumed that the standards of practical reason can be understood apart from ethical virtue, and that the question "Why should I be moral?" is about how the life of ethical virtue, and moral virtue in particular—the life of justice and benevolence—is to be justified by these standards.[8]

This is true most obviously of the instrumentalist approach, on which good practical thought is finding and taking the means to one's ends, where the ends are set by brute desire. No doubt a virtuous person is good at doing these things. But, on the face of it, the converse implication does not hold. One need not have the virtues of character in order to be good at getting what one wants. And if one is selfish but efficient, the virtues of justice and benevolence may seem to get in the way.

As this suggests, the question of reasons to be moral will be pressing also for those who tie *self-interest* to practical reason, insisting that an agent should do only what will benefit her. Why should she keep a promise, or restrain her appetites, unless she stands to gain by doing so? Some have argued—in the spirit of Hobbes' *Leviathan*—that the moral virtues *can* be justified in terms of self-interest or desire. These arguments are controversial, either because they seem to justify too little, or because they only show the benefits of being just or benevolent in general, not in every particular case.[9] But these issues are beside the point. The argument of

---

[7] For the idiom of "consistency in action," see O'Neill (1985) and Gibbard (1999).

[8] See Brink (1992) for an elegant account of this debate; an important precursor is Foot (1972).

[9] For an argument that falls into the first trap, see Gauthier (1986); for the second, see Foot (1958–9).

this book is directed not only against those for whom the contrast between reason and virtue amounts to actual divergence, but also to many of those who hope to see them coincide. The question is whether the standards of practical reason can be so much as understood apart from ethical virtue, so that it is the task of a more or less elaborate argument to bring them back into line. In my view, the project of *Leviathan*, and projects like it, are misconceived right from the start. They wrongly assume that we can explain what practical reason is in terms of self-interest or the satisfaction of desire—and in isolation from the virtues of character.

A distinction of the same kind is implicit even in Kantian conceptions of practical reason, which aspire to demonstrate the rational authority of the moral law. In doing so, they begin with the nature of agency or practical thought, from which they hope to derive "internal" or "constitutive" standards of success. It follows that, even if the Kantian argument shows that we *should* be benevolent and just, the most it can be is a vindication of the virtues of character in terms of practical reason, *independently conceived*. It is the assumption of independence that I oppose.

It is already clear, in this sketch of my conclusion, that I am engaged in a kind of "virtue ethics." I am happy to accept that description; but it could be misleading. Virtue ethics is many things to many people, and only some of them are at issue here. It will be helpful, then, to locate my project briefly within the space of ethical theories that appeal to the virtues of character.

I have three things, primarily, in mind: virtue ethics as concerned with moral perception, and hostile to moral principles; virtue ethics as competing with consequentialism and deontology; and virtue ethics as Aristotelian naturalism. This book does not fit squarely in any of these conceptions; its topic is virtue ethics as a theory of practical reason.

There is, nevertheless, some overlap, particularly with the first conception: virtue ethics as (what has come to be called) "particularism."[10] There are in fact two questions here, not always clearly distinguished. On the one hand, there is the question whether the content of morality, or of practical reason more generally, can be codified in non-ethical terms—for instance, whether we can express, with a finite non-moral description, the conditions of application of every moral concept. One kind of generalist says that we can. One kind of particularist denies it: he claims that the class of things that fall under a moral concept may be "shapeless" at the level of non-moral description. On the other hand, there is a question about the role of ethical principles in the practical thought of the ethically

---

[10] On particularism in ethics, see, especially, McDowell (1979), Wallace (1991), and the papers in Hooker and Little (2000).

virtuous person: does she decide what to do by applying a set of principles to the situation at hand? These questions are obviously connected: if the content of morality or practical reason cannot be codified in non-ethical terms, there is a kind of principle on which the virtuous person cannot rely, simply because there is no such thing. But the questions are nonetheless distinct. It might be possible to capture the content of ethics in finite terms, without its being true that knowledge of this description figures in the psychology of ethical virtue. Nothing I say in this book will bear in a direct way on the first question, about the existence of finite principles. But I will argue for a sceptical position about the need for ethical principles, of almost any kind, in the practical thought involved in the virtues of character.[11]

I will have less to say about the other conceptions of virtue ethics. According to one of them, virtue ethics is to be conceived as an alternative to consequentialism and deontology.[12] Consequentialists want to define right action in terms of "the good"—the idea of a good outcome or state of affairs. The right action is that which generates the most good, or a sufficient amount of good. Deontologists define the good in terms of right action, or at least reject the consequentialist definition of the latter. In contrast with both views, virtue theorists (of the relevant kind) hope to explain right action, and the good, in terms of ethical virtue. Each of these theories is characterized by a claim of "*explanatory primacy*" (Watson 1990: 451).

I want to distance myself from this, in two ways. First, to repeat a point I have already made, my topic is not morality in a narrow sense, but ethics in general. I am not interested in what makes an action *morally* right or wrong, in particular, but in what one should do, all things considered. And I leave room for non-moral virtues. Second, although I am arguing for a metaphysical connection between ethical virtue and practical reason, I do not claim that the connection is *asymmetric* in any interesting way. We can say what it is to be a reason for action in terms of ethical virtue, or so I will claim. But that is not to say that the virtues of character have explanatory primacy. The connection between reason and virtue runs in both directions: it is a matter of reciprocity, not priority.

This fact is worth stressing, and I return to it below, and in the conclusion of the book. For now, two further points. The first depends on being careful about the distinction between metaphysics and epistemology. Even if it were true, in some sense, that ethical virtue is more basic than practical reason in the metaphysical order of explanation, it would not follow—and I do not believe—that it is epistemically prior. It would not

---

[11] See Part Two, section 1.

[12] For a classic expression of this approach, see Watson (1990) building on Rawls (1970).

follow that claims about what there is reason to do must always be derived from claims about ethical virtue that are antecedently justified, or
that the order of justification cannot go the other way.[13] If reason and
virtue are connected in the way that I propose, assumptions about practical reason might be used to prove conclusions about the virtues of character—though the converse holds as well.

The second point is also connected with issues of metaphysical explanation. On the third conception mentioned above, virtue ethics is identified with Aristotelian naturalism, according to which we can explain
what a human virtue is in terms of human nature, human flourishing, or
the human function.[14] It is often taken for granted that an account of
this kind is necessary. But that assumption is mistaken, in at least two
ways. First, we should not forget that the Aristotelian tradition is only
one possibility here; there is also the "sentimentalist" virtue ethics of
Hutcheson and Hume, with its radically different view of the metaphysics and epistemology of virtue. Second, even those who appeal to Aristotle do not always agree that his naturalism has explanatory ambitions.
In "The Role of *Eudaimonia* in Aristotle's Ethics," John McDowell argues that "disputes [about what one should do] could evidently be
conducted as disputes about what it is the business of a human being to
do" (1980: 13). But there is no suggestion that the justification for claims
about "the business of a human being is to be found in an independent,
'value-free' investigation of human nature." On the contrary, the
reference to "human nature" here is "a sort of rhetorical flourish, added
to a conclusion already complete without it" (1980: 19). In effect, Mc-
Dowell reads Aristotle as a quietist or anti-foundationalist about human
virtue.

It does not matter for my purposes whether McDowell is right about
this, or exactly what his doctrine amounts to—though, like him, I want
to resist the bad idea that the *reasons* for being virtuous turn on an appeal
to self-interest or human nature.[15] What matters is that our investigation
of virtue and practical reason does not depend on any particular view
about the metaphysics of virtue. It is, I think, compatible with the senti-
mentalism of Hume's *Treatise* and with the naturalism or quietism—
whichever it is—of the *Nicomachean Ethics*. On these metaphysical questions, my argument is basically silent.

[13] On antecedent justification, see Pryor (2000).
[14] For accounts of this kind, see Thompson (1995)—following Anscombe (1958: 38,
41)—MacIntyre (1999), Hursthouse (1999, Part III), and Foot (2001).
[15] For a reading of Aristotle that may fall into this trap, see Williams (1985, ch. 3). Mc-
Dowell (1980; 1995b, §§2–3) and Watson (1990) argue, in different ways, that virtue ethics
should not be conceived on an egoistic model. See also Hurka (2001, ch. 8).

In the rest of this introduction, I attempt to do two things. In section 1, I clarify and make precise the claim about reason and virtue that the rest of the book defends. In doing so, I solve a problem for virtue ethics that has seemed decisive to some: an argument by Bernard Williams that it makes no sense for the less-than-virtuous to imitate the fully virtuous person.[16] If this is right, it is not clear how the virtue theorist can state the connection between ethical virtue and reasons for us to act. Responding to Williams, I explain how this connection can be made. In section 2, I sketch the argument of the book as a whole. It begins with a theory of action developed in Part One, which figures as a premise in the argument about reason and virtue that occupies Part Two.

1. "Squeezing the Good into the Right through the Tubes of Imperfection"

According to Aristotle, we engage in deliberation "where the outcome is unclear and the right way to act is undefined" (*NE* 1112b9–11).[17] Here "deliberation" seems to mean something *active* or *intentional*, the kind of deliberative thought in which we deliberately engage, surveying our circumstance and what we can do to change or affect it. As Aristotle says, we engage in active deliberation mostly when our decision is difficult— though it need not be important. Much of our time is spent acting intentionally but without deliberating, in this sense: we get out of bed, make breakfast, and go to work, often without so much as wondering why.

Aristotle also said that "what is decided is what has been previously deliberated" (*NE* 1112a15–16), and he apparently means that every decision (*prohairesis*) is a product of deliberation. It is obvious at once that there is a problem here. If deliberation is something we do intentionally, and if "decision" has its ordinary meaning, then it seems wrong to say that every decision depends on prior deliberation. Indeed, it *must* be wrong, since it would initiate a vicious regress in which even the decision to deliberate would have to be deliberated in turn.

What we need here is a concept of deliberation that applies even when the thinking behind an action is not itself intentional. In fact, it will be useful to cast our net more widely than that. I want to count as "practical thought" or "practical reasoning"—terms I use interchangeably—not only deliberation as an intentional action, but the motivation of action done for reasons (though perhaps without deliberation, in the strict

---

[16] The argument appears in Williams (1995a: 189–90).

[17] I use Irwin's (1999) translation of the *Nicomachean Ethics*, with occasional transliteration of the Greek. The title of this section is taken from Williams (1995a: 190).

sense), the balancing of reasons (even when it is not conscious), and the forming and revising of intentions and desires. There is no perfectly natural phrase for the topic I have in mind. "Practical thought" may suggest something wholly cognitive, a matter of evaluative belief, or thoughts about what there is good reason to do. We should not assume that practical thought in the broad sense must always include such things, and it certainly is not exhausted by them. "Practical reasoning" may suggest some kind of *calculation*, perhaps about the means to one's ends.[18] But the practical thought involved in acting for a reason, for instance, need not involve calculation in any ordinary sense, and we should not assume at the outset that it must depend on our desires. Finally, both "practical thought" and "practical reasoning" may suggest a restriction to mental goings-on, things that terminate with desires or intentions to act, not with action itself.[19] I want to count *acting* for a reason as a central instance of practical thought. After all, it is relevant to one's degree of responsiveness to reason whether one merely forms the intention to act, about which one is then weak-willed, or whether one actually tries to do something about it.[20]

The principal topic of this book is practical thought, understood in this broad and somewhat artificial sense. The virtue theory of practical reason is a claim about what constitutes *good* practical thought. But since virtues are traits of character, it is more readily framed in terms of our *dispositions* to engage in practical thought, or what I will simply call "dispositions of practical thought." A disposition of practical thought is good, as such, just in case it is a disposition to engage in good practical thought. According to the virtue theory, the property of being good as a disposition of practical thought can also be explained in terms of virtue.

> *The Virtue Theory*: Being good as a disposition of practical thought is being a disposition of practical thought that is good as a trait of character.

There are several things to clarify here. First, this is meant to be a claim of *identity*, on which the property of being good as a disposition of practical thought just *is* the property of being good as a trait of character, applied to dispositions of practical thought. A consequence is that one's dispositions of practical thought are good, as such, just in case (and just to the extent that) they are good as traits of character. Second, we need to say

---

[18] For the suggestion about calculation, see Anscombe (1963: 65), following Aristotle (*NE* 1139a12–15).

[19] For this restriction, see Broome (2001: 175).

[20] On weakness of will, see, especially, Holton (1999). In stipulating that acting for a reason is a kind of practical thought, I take no stand on the substantive issues, if any, raised by Aristotle's doctrine that action is the conclusion of practical syllogism.

more about the dispositions that constitute good character: what is the psychology of ethical virtue? That will have to wait until Part Two, in "Character and Practical Thought." (More generally, that section examines the detailed application of the virtue theory.) Third, we want to know what the virtue theorist says, not only about our dispositions of practical thought, but about our reasons to act. It is sometimes said that virtue ethics will face a decisive problem here; in the rest of this section, I argue that it does not.

I began this book with the fundamental question of ethics: "How should one live?" And I took this to be a question about *reasons*: "What is there most reason to do?" "Reasons," here, are considerations that count in favour. Reasons for doing something are considerations that count in favour of doing it; reasons for caring about someone are considerations that count in favour of caring. So, for instance, the fact that it is a beautiful day is a reason for me to quit work early; the fact that this is my child is a reason for me to care about him; and so on. In claims like these, reasons are facts that support or tend to justify an attitude or a course of action, for a particular person in a particular context. There is a risk of ambiguity here, since we talk about people's reasons for doing things without assuming that their reasons are good. There is a distinction between the use of "reason" in *explaining* someone's action, or attitude, and its use as a term for *justification*—although they are surely connected. We will examine the explanation of action by reasons in Part One. For the moment, we are interested in practical justification: we are interested in *ethics*, and the "should" that signifies what there is most reason to do.

The problem is that, while it is possible to state the virtue theory as a claim about dispositions of practical thought, as above, it is not clear how to relate the virtues of character, or the ethically virtuous person, to reasons for acting or the ethical sense of "should." Bernard Williams (1995a: 189–90) has argued, influentially, that this puzzle amounts to a fatal flaw: one's reasons are sensitive to one's defects of character in a way that prevents them from being understood in virtue-theoretic terms. His target is the tempting formulation that I employed, with caveats, at the beginning of this book: that one should live and act as a person of good character would live and act in one's place. To reason well in practical matters is to reason in ways that are characteristic of those who have the virtues of character, "someone like Aristotle's *phronimos*, [. . .] someone who has been properly brought up" (Williams 1995a: 189). Taking the virtuous person as a standard, we are led to a proposal that looks like this:

(V) The fact that p is a reason for A to ϕ just in case A would be moved to ϕ by the belief that p, at least to some extent, if she had the virtues of character.

the problem of imitation

However tempting it may be, this formulation is deeply flawed. For one thing, it assumes that the virtues of character are mutually compatible, and that may not be so. But there is a further and more fundamental problem. As Williams has shown, it is a mistake to explain the idea of a reason for acting in *imitative* terms.

> [According to (V)] what A has reason to do in certain circumstances is what the *phronimos* would have reason to do in those circumstances. But, in considering what he has reason to do, one thing that A should take into account, if he is grown up and has some sense, are the ways in which he relevantly fails to be a *phronimos*. Aristotle's *phronimos* (to stay with that model) was, for instance, supposed to display temperance, a moderate equilibrium of the passions which did not even require the emergency semi-virtue of self-control. But, if I know that I fall short of temperance and am unreliable with respect even to some kinds of self-control, I shall have good reason not to do some things that a temperate person could properly and safely do. (Williams 1995a: 190)

To take an example from Watson (1975: 210), which is used by Michael Smith (1995: 110–1) in a similar context, suppose that I have just lost a very hard game of squash to an infuriating opponent. In this circumstance, the virtuous person would calmly shake his opponent's hand. But if I were to attempt that, I would fly into a rage and beat him with my racquet. The fact that I have a short fuse is a reason for me to take a cold shower, but it is not a reason by which I would need to be motivated if I had the virtues of character. In a circumstance like this, (V) gets it wrong: it cannot accommodate the reasons I have that would not be reasons for the *phronimos*, in a similar place.

The example depends on my having a defect of character, and on this defect's being practically significant. So perhaps our mistake was not to build this defect into the specification of my circumstance, before relating it to (V). But this won't help:

> It will be no good trying to accommodate this difficulty, of squeezing the good into the right through the tubes of imperfection, by putting all A's limitations in the account of the circumstances. If the circumstances are defined partly in terms of the agent's ethical imperfection, then the *phronimos* cannot be in *those* circumstances and [(V)] cannot apply at all. (Williams 1995a: 190)

Since defects of character can be relevant to my circumstance in ways that bear on what I have reason to do, there is simply no way to explain those reasons in terms of the practical reasoning of the virtuous person who finds himself in exactly the circumstance that I am in.

Williams' argument is, I think, a decisive objection to (V). What is striking about it, however, is that it does not depend essentially on appeal to the virtues of character. The point of the argument is really quite general:

it is about imitation, not ethical virtue. If I am bad at practical reasoning, whatever that amounts to, I am bound to have reasons that do not apply to those whose dispositions of practical thought are better than mine. So the problem for (V) is just as much a problem for (R):

(R) The fact that p is a reason for A to ϕ just in case A would be moved to ϕ by the belief that p, at least to some extent, if her dispositions of practical thought were perfectly good.

Suppose that I am prone to a failure of practical reason: I tend to give too much weight to sunk costs. That will affect what there is reason for me to do, providing me with reasons that I would not have if my dispositions of practical thought were flawlessly good. For instance, it may be my heart's desire to run a successful restaurant, but my obsession with sunk costs will get in the way. If I open a restaurant, and try to make a go of it, I will be unable to back out: unable to quit when things are hopeless, even though it would be self-destructive to go on. The fact that opening a restaurant is such a risky prospect, that most restaurants fail, and that pouring in more money doesn't help—these may be reasons for *me* not to do it, even though they would not apply to someone who did not share my defect of practical thought. The problem here is exactly parallel to the one that Williams describes.

What this shows is that we have misunderstood the relationship between practical reasons and practical reasoning, in general. The problem of imitation does not depend on an alleged connection between practical reason and virtue of character; it is not a problem about virtue at all. It is about the need for care in stating the formal connection between reasons for action and good dispositions of practical thought, whatever their content may be. Our mistake was to connect particular reasons for action with the case in which someone has the whole array of good dispositions. In doing so, we necessarily obscure the way in which reasons can depend on defects of practical thought. Still, it is clear that there must be some connection here. It would make no sense to conclude that the standards of practical thought are conceptually independent of the facts about reasons to act. The only question is how to state their relation to one another. And this is a question for everyone—not just for those who are sympathetic to the virtue theory of practical reason.

Roughly speaking, the connection seems to be this: a reason is a premise for an episode of good practical thought whose other conditions are already in place. If the fact that p is a reason for you to ϕ, then it is good practical thought to be moved to ϕ by a certain array of psychological states, and you have that array—except, perhaps, for the belief that p. This belief would supply the final material for a good disposition of practical thought. We can make this idea more precise as follows:

Reasons: The fact that *p* is a reason for A to φ just in case A has a collection of psychological states, C, such that the disposition to be moved to φ by C-and-the-belief-that-*p* is a good disposition of practical thought, and C contains no false beliefs.[21]

The last clause of this formula—"no false beliefs"—is required to deal with a final difficulty. In an earlier example, which I have slightly modified, Williams imagines a thirsty person, presented with what seems to be a glass of cool, refreshing water (1980: 102). In fact, the glass contains odourless petrol. If I am in this situation, is the fact that I am thirsty a reason for me to drink the contents of the glass? As Williams says, the answer would seem to be "no." If the glass contains petrol, the fact that I am thirsty is no reason to drink from it, at all; there is no good reason to drink what is in the glass. The inclination to say otherwise turns on the fact that I have a collection of psychological states—including the belief that the glass contains water—such that the disposition to be moved to drink by them, together with the belief that I am thirsty, is a good disposition of practical thought. What the example shows is that good practical thought corresponds to reasons only when it involves no false beliefs.[22] A consequence of this refined claim is that our reasons

---

[21] It is worth comparing this claim briefly with a different solution to something like the generalized problem of imitation: the "advice model" proposed by Michael Smith. His central claim is that "[what] we have reason to do in the circumstances in which we find ourselves is fixed by the advice our fully rational selves would give us about what to do in these circumstances" (Smith 1995: 112). Advice is cashed out in terms of *desire*; so reasons correspond, not to the motivations we would *have* if we were "fully rational," but to the motivations we would *want* ourselves to have, in our actual position. This model assumes—I think, quite dubiously—that those who are "fully rational" must be good at giving advice. That may be true, but it is far from trivial: it is like the assumption of those who treat Prince Myshkin as a mentor, in Dostoevsky's *The Idiot* (1869). (For a similar objection, see Millgram 1996: 218, n. 14.) In any case, there is a fundamental difference between the advice model and the claim defended in the text. My account is concerned with the connection between reasons for action and good practical thought in the circumstance in which they apply. The advice model, by contrast, relates the reasons of an agent to the practical thought of his *advisor*. It does not say anything, for its own part, about the standards of practical thought that apply to the circumstance the agent is in. Thus, even if the advice model is true—which I doubt—it does not explain the connection we have been looking for, the connection I said there simply must be, between practical reasons and the quality of the practical thought that takes those reasons into account.

[22] A natural question to ask at this point is: why not correct for *ignorance* as well as false belief? But that "correction" would be a mistake. Reasons for action *may* correspond to practical thought that depends on ignorance of fact. So, for instance, there may be a reason for the gambler to bet on the horse with the best odds, even though it will lose the race—since he does not *know* that the horse will lose. His reason corresponds to good practical thought that depends essentially on his being in the dark about that. (For this example, attributed to Frank Jackson, see Dancy 2000: 65–6.)

supervene on our psychological states, together with the truth of our beliefs. The rest of the world is irrelevant. If agents are psychological duplicates, and their beliefs are similarly true or false, then their reasons must be the same.[23]

The doctrine of *Reasons* is immune to the problem of imitation because it does not connect the assessment of practical thought with the case in which *all* of one's dispositions are good. If the risk of failure is a reason not to open a restaurant, since I give too much weight to sunk costs, the disposition to be deterred by that consideration in my imperfect circumstance is a good disposition of practical thought. (More carefully, I ought to be deterred to some extent; not all reasons are decisive ones.) This is true even though I would not be deterred if I had the whole array of good dispositions.

As with the virtue theory, *Reasons* should be thought of as basically symmetric. It says that we can move from claims about reasons to claims about good dispositions of practical thought, and back again. It does not imply that claims of the latter kind have metaphysical or epistemic priority.[24] And it can therefore be accepted by non-reductionists about reasons, and by those for whom good practical thought involves knowledge of what there is reason to do.

We can state a similar claim about the *relative weight* of reasons to act:

> Reasons correspond to collections of psychological states that fuel good practical thought. One reason is *stronger* than another just in case it is a good disposition of practical thought to be *more strongly moved* by the collection of states that corresponds to it, than by the collection that corresponds to the other.

(Here, "good" means "better than the alternative," not "fine" or "good enough." We would otherwise permit the impossible case in which two reasons are stronger than each other, because the corresponding and conflicting dispositions are both "good enough.") With this principle in hand, we can finally explain the relationship between what one should do, all things considered, and the assessment of practical thought. What one should do is determined by the balance of reasons, which is fixed in turn by the relative weight of all the reasons there are. The facts about reasons correspond, in the ways I have been describing, to facts about good dispositions of practical thought.

---

[23] This claim is stronger than Scanlon's (1998: 73–4) "universality of reason judgments," but it is in the same vein.

[24] There is the following asymmetry: all reasons correspond to good dispositions of practical thought, but good dispositions need not correspond to reasons, since they may not take the relevant form—that of a disposition to be moved to *act* by, among other things, a *belief*.

None of this depends on the virtue theory of practical reason. Although it began as a question about reason and virtue, we have seen that the problem of imitation is entirely general: it applies to (R) as much as (V). In solving it, we have to articulate more carefully the formal connection between reasons for action and good dispositions of practical thought. That there *is* such a connection is something everyone should accept. What the virtue theory adds is a distinctive conception of what is good in practical thought: not efficiency, or practical consistency, but virtue of character. Being good as a disposition of practical thought is being a disposition of practical thought that is good as a trait of character. Since the facts about reasons correspond to facts about good dispositions of practical thought, the virtue theory can serve as a theory of reasons, and of what one *should* do, all things considered. As I remarked before, this is not a claim of metaphysical or epistemic priority. I am not saying that facts about good dispositions are more basic than facts about reasons, in any significant way. If the virtue theory is right, we can move seamlessly from practical reason to ethical virtue, and the reverse.

2. The Relevance of Action Theory

This book presents a single sustained argument for the virtue theory of practical reason. It is inspired by an ominous pronouncement in Elizabeth Anscombe's "Modern Moral Philosophy":

> [It] is not profitable for us at present to do moral philosophy; that should be laid aside at any rate until we have an adequate philosophy of psychology, in which we are conspicuously lacking. (Anscombe 1958: 26)

Times have changed—not, I will argue, because it is any more profitable to engage in philosophical ethics apart from the philosophy of mind, but because we have Anscombe's work on which to draw. In the year before she wrote the words I have quoted here, Anscombe published the first edition of *Intention*, that difficult and remarkable book. Although I will criticize her work, below, its influence on my approach is deep. Like Anscombe, I think we cannot understand the character of practical reason without an account of what it is to act. More carefully, we need an account of what it is to act *intentionally*, and what it is to act for a reason. These are the questions to be explored in Part One.

In turning from ethics to action theory, I follow not only Anscombe, but a family of views in moral philosophy that may be gathered together under the heading of "ethical rationalism." According to the rationalist, in this sense of the term, the standards of practical reason can be derived, at least in outline, from the nature of agency or practical thought. The

philosophy of action is thus the foundation of ethics. The most prom
rationalist views belong to the tradition that descends from Kant, and ..
use of the term derives from and extends its application there. We find
versions of Kantian rationalism in recent work by David Velleman (*Practical Reflection, The Possibility of Practical Reason*) and Christine Korsgaard (*The Sources of Normativity*).[25] For instance, Velleman claims that
we can say what it is to act intentionally in terms of a "constitutive aim,"
something to which everything we do is tacitly directed. Right action is
what best achieves this constitutive aim. For Korsgaard, the standards of
practical reason follow from the fact that rational agency depends on
reflective endorsement. Right action must be compatible with *unconditional* endorsement and thus, so the argument runs, with respect for humanity as an end in itself. Understood in a schematic way, however, the
project of ethical rationalism is not compelled to take a Kantian form.
For instance, it appears in the version of *instrumentalism* on which desire-
satisfaction is the goal of practical reason because desire has a distinctive
place in practical thought.[26] On this view, too, the standards of practical
reason derive from the nature of agency, as such.

Although I share the rationalist concern with agency, I do not share its
optimism. One of the central arguments of this book is that the standards
of practical reason *cannot* be derived from the nature of agency or practical thought, not even in outline, or in general terms. As I will try to show,
it follows from this failure that the virtue theory is true. The reasoning
here is hard to summarize; it depends on a premise about the metaphysics
of *being good* that I defend in the second section of Part Two, "An Argument for the Virtue Theory." But the upshot is this: those who reject the
virtue theory of practical reason *must* accept some form of ethical rationalism. They must derive the standards of practical reason, at least in
outline, from the nature of agency or practical thought. (This is so even
if, like the instrumentalist, they do not take a traditionally Kantian line.)
If ethical rationalism is false, as I argue it is, then the virtue theory must
be true. The standards of practical reason are standards of good character,
applied to practical thought.

This sketch leaves much to be filled in. Why should the metaphysics of
being good force us to choose between rationalism and the virtue theory?
How do the standards of good character apply to practical thought? What
is wrong with ethical rationalism? These questions will be answered in
Part Two. In the rest of this introduction, I want to say more about Part
One, and the role it plays in the arguments to come.

---

[25] Velleman (1989; 2000b); Korsgaard (1996); see also Nagel (1970) and Railton (1997).
[26] See Williams (1980); Dreier (1997).

The topic of Part One is the claim that we act intentionally *sub specie boni*: "under the guise of the good." On this "normative" conception of agency, to do something intentionally is to see some good in doing it; and to act for a reason is to act on a belief one takes to justify what one does, at least to some extent. As I will argue later on, this picture of agency is presupposed by the Kantian rationalist. But it is more widely shared. The same conception is at work in some Platonic and Aristotelian views, and it is often unreflectively assumed. I will try to show that it is false. In fact, one way to understand the argument of the book as a whole is to think of it as working out the consequences for practical reason of rejecting the claim that we act under the guise of the good.

We need to make some distinctions here. The normative conception of agency may derive from a doctrine about desire: "[what] is required for our concept of 'wanting' is that a man should see what he wants under the aspect of some good. [. . .] The conceptual connexion between 'wanting' [. . .] and 'good' can be compared to the conceptual connexion between 'judgement' and 'truth'" (Anscombe 1963: 75–6).[27] If an agent must *want* to do what he intentionally does, it will follow that he must see what he is doing "under the aspect of some good." (A slightly different view is possible here, on which it is one's *intention* to act that involves, or is identified with, an evaluative judgement.)[28] Although I will mention these claims, below, what interests me most of all is an alleged connection between good or normative reasons—"reasons" in the sense of section 1—and the reasons for which we act. Although it is obvious that we can act for bad reasons, it is commonly held that we must at least *believe* that the reasons for which we act are good, that they are considerations that count in favour of what we are doing: "to say that a factor is the agent's reason is to claim that the agent decided that it was a sufficient reason or sufficient grounds for acting in the way he did" (Milligan 1974: 183); an agent who acts for reasons "is *guided* by reason, and in particular, guided by what reason presents as necessary" (Korsgaard 1997: 221). (The quoted claims are excessively strong. A more modest view is that one must regard one's reason as doing *something* to justify one's action, even if it is not sufficient.)[29] More generally, deciding what to do is often assumed to be a matter of deciding what

[27] For similar claims, see Stampe (1987) and Tenenbaum (2003). The evaluative conception of desire is criticized by Stocker (1979) and Velleman (1992), among others.

[28] See Davidson (1978: 98–99); this picture of intention lies behind the problem of *akrasia*, as it appears in Davidson (1970a).

[29] For the claim that acting for a reason is acting for what one takes to be a *good* reason, see also Darwall (1983: 205), Bond (1983: 30–1), Walker (1989: 670), Broome (1997), Raz (1997: 8, 1999), Wallace (1999), Velleman (1992a: 101, 1992b: 140–2, 2000b: 9), and many others. A similar view is held by Anscombe (1963: 21–5).

it would be good, or even best, to do.[30] And descriptions of practical thought quite commonly imply that, in weighing reasons, one "come[s] to see that [one] has reason to do something" (Williams 1980: 104), as though responding to reasons were always a matter of making judgements that deploy the concept of justification. In coming to act upon the reasons we have weighed, "[the] basic case [is] that in which A ϕ's [. . .] because he believes of some determinate consideration that it constitutes a reason for him to ψ" (Williams 1980: 107).

In my view, all of these claims are false, and false not merely in marginal cases, where an agent is being irrational or suffers from *akrasia*, but in quite ordinary ones, as well. There is a sense in which, in acting for a reason, one must see the consideration on which one acts *as* one's reason for acting, but one need not see it as a *good* reason for acting, a reason in the normative or justifying sense. To clarify: it is not just that one need not see the consideration as *sufficient* reason; one need not see it as doing anything at all to justify what one does. This claim about agency will be the primary conclusion of Part One.

It supports a further claim about practical thought, in general. As I will argue in Part Two, if we do not act under the guise of the good, there is no reason to suppose that practical thought depends on evaluative judgement. Acting as one should may be the formal object of practical reason, in the sense explained above, in section 1, but it is not the material object of practical thought. We can engage in practical reasoning, and act on it, without asking whether the reasons for which we are acting are any good. We may decide to live like Countess Gemini, in *The Portrait of a Lady*, who cheerfully insists, "I don't care anything about reasons, but I know what I like" (James 1881: 307). But even this gives the wrong impression, that those who do not *reflect* about reasons are wanton or reckless in some way. That need not be so: even the virtuous person may not be articulate; she may not be able to say, and may not even have considered, why what she is doing is right.[31]

The arguments described so far belong to action theory, or moral psychology. What do they have to do with ethics and practical reason? In effect, that is the topic of Part Two. Its principal *negative* claim is that we cannot derive the content of practical reason, not even in outline, from the nature of agency or practical thought—and for reasons that depend upon the arguments of Part One. The project of ethical rationalism turns out quite often to rely upon the guise of the good. Thus, advocates of

---

[30] Watson: "Practical deliberation, as I think of it, is *reasoning about what is best (or satisfactory) to do with a view to making up one's mind about what to do*" (2003: 175).

[31] In thinking about this fact, I have been influenced by Iris Murdoch; see, especially, Murdoch (1970: 2, 51–2). I say more about this in Part Two, section 1.

Kantian rationalism have typically assumed that, in acting for reasons, we aim to *justify* what we do. That is their mistake. The same point holds for the "recognitional" conception of practical reason, on which practical thought is thought about what there is reason to do, and for what might be called "Aristotelian rationalism." I explain and criticize these views in Part Two, section 3.

The arguments of Part One are relevant even to forms of ethical rationalism that do not depend upon the guise of the good. (Think, for instance, of the instrumentalist view that practical thought is always directed by desire, so that its aim is desire-satisfaction; or the attempt to derive the standards of practical reason from the fact that, in acting for reasons, we know what we are doing and why.)[32] By defending a positive theory of action, I hope to show, in general, that there is no room for the rationalist project to succeed. If the arguments of Part One are right, there is *nothing* in the nature of action, or of practical thought, from which the standards of practical reason could derive. The only alternative—so I claim in Part Two—is that the virtue theory is true.

This is still schematic, and the details will have to wait. But it is already enough to provoke a response. To many, the strategy of this book will seem ironic. It is a defence of virtue ethics that depends on the claim that we do not act under the guise of the good. But the guise of the good is a doctrine that descends from, and is an intimate part of, the dominant tradition of virtue ethics, the one that begins with Socrates, and flows through Plato, Aristotle, and Aquinas, to Anscombe and to us. This is not an accident. While the influence of Aristotle should be apparent here, it is overshadowed by the influence of Hume.

This may seem surprising. While Hume's interest in virtue is obvious, he has usually been read as an instrumentalist about practical reason: a passion may be "call'd unreasonable" just in case "[it is] founded on a false supposition, or when it chooses means insufficient for the design'd end" (*Treatise* 2.3.3.7).[33] "Reason is, and ought only to be, the slave of passions" (2.3.3.4). This take on Hume is so widespread that it is often made true by definition: in much of the literature, "Humean" just *means* instrumentalist. More recently, some critics have urged that Hume is a *sceptic* about practical reason: he rejects its would-be standards, including

---

[32] It is natural to read Williams as attempting to derive a broadly instrumentalist conception of practical reason from the role of desire in practical thought (1980). See also Dreier (1997). Velleman derives a theory of reasons for action from the cognitive content of intending to act (1989, 2000b). I criticize these views towards the end of Part Two.

[33] Hume (1739–40). I cite the *Treatise* in the main text by giving book, part, section and paragraph numbers.

the standard of instrumental reason, outright.[34] After all, he argues that it is "*impossible* [. . .] that [a] passion can be oppos'd to, or be contradictory to truth and reason" (2.3.3.5, my emphasis). This is how he comes to write one of the most arresting passages in his work:

> 'Tis not contrary to reason to prefer the destruction of the world to the scratching of my finger. 'Tis not contrary to reason for me to choose my total ruin, to prevent the least uneasiness of an *Indian* or person wholly unknown to me. 'Tis as little contrary to reason to prefer even my own acknowledg'd lesser good to my greater, and have a more ardent affection for the former than the latter. (2.3.3.6)

Hume is not, however, an instrumentalist or a sceptic. This is not the place in which to argue this at length.[35] The views that occupy this book are not meant as an interpretation of Hume, and do not correspond to his, except in a general way. What I take from him is an idea that lies behind the treatment of reason and passion in the *Treatise*: we know what we mean by "theoretical reason" or "reason, in a strict and philosophical sense" (3.1.1.12); but we have no clear conception of a "practical reason" that corresponds to this. We do not know what practical reason *is*, if it is meant to provide a standard for thought and action, apart from the standards of virtue and vice.

This means that there is a sense in which Hume *is* a sceptic about practical reason, as the passage above suggests. But the sense is limited: he is a sceptic about practical reason, I think, only on a rationalist account of what it must be. For Hume, ethical rationalism is the attempt to model practical on theoretical reason, and it comes in the end to a confusion of the two. When this confusion is cleared away, Hume finds it misleading, rather than helpful, to apply the term "reason" in ethics at all; he wants to limit its use to "reason, in a strict and philosophical sense." And so his language is that of a sceptic: "reason alone can never be a motive to any action of the will" (2.3.3.1); nor can our passions conflict with it. Ethical virtue is left as the only intelligible standard for action and practical thought.

My arguments are not the same as Hume's. There is at most a loose correspondence between the rationalism of the British moralists and the kind of rationalism that figures in this book—a kind that does not confuse practical with theoretical reason. Nor do I sympathize with Hume's refusal to speak of "reason" in ethics if, as he concludes, a rationalist account is false. To believe in practical reason is simply to believe that there are things that we should do, and reasons for doing them—and however

---

[34] See Hampton (1995), Millgram (1995), and Korsgaard (1997).
[35] I have done so in Setiya (2004c).

he would put the point, Hume surely agrees with that. His scruples about "reason, in a strict and philosophical sense" tend to obscure the best insight of his argument, that there is nothing for reason to *be*, in ethics, if it is not a matter of good character. That is my view too. Like Hume, on this admittedly tendentious reading, I argue that we must interpret the ethical "should" in terms of ethical virtue, because no other interpretation makes sense.

PART ONE

Explaining Action

ACCORDING to an ancient tradition of thought about human action, whatever we do intentionally is done "under the guise of the good": we must see something worthwhile in what we are doing—though we may of course be wrong about it. This idea finds its strictest expression in the infamous Socratic doctrine that no one errs willingly.[1] But it survives in the *Republic* too: "Every soul pursues the good and does whatever it does for its sake" (505e).[2] There are complications here, in Plato's account of non-rational (appetitive and spirited) desires.[3] But he surely saw some grain of truth in a qualified version of Socrates' claim. The same can be said of Aristotle, whose *Nicomachean Ethics* begins with the following declaration:

> Every craft and every line of inquiry, and likewise every action and decision, seems to seek some good; that is why some people were right to describe the good as what everything seeks. (*NE* 1094a1–4)

And in the moral psychology of *De Anima*, "it is always the object of desire which produces movement, [and] this is either good or the apparent good" (433a27–29).[4]

Perhaps none of these claims corresponds precisely to the one I will address, and argue against, in this part of the book. But it surely descends from them, and seems to inherit whatever plausibility they have. The doctrine I have in mind is that *reasons for action* must be seen under the guise of the good. We can act for bad reasons, on this view, but we must at least *regard* our reasons as good, as doing something to justify our action. This relatively modest claim might serve as common ground not only for those mentioned above, but for Aquinas and the scholastic philosophers influenced by him, and even for Kant. Whatever else it may involve, Kant's argument from freedom to the moral law assumes that rational beings aim to justify their choices. That is why transcendental freedom, uncon-

---

[1] See, especially, Plato's *Protagoras*, *Meno*, and *Gorgias*. This theme is brilliantly discussed in Segvic (2000).

[2] The translation is by Grube and Reeve, from Cooper's (1997) edition of Plato.

[3] For instance, at *Republic* 438a ff., Plato seems to describe the appetite of thirst as a desire for drink, as such—not as *good*. But the passage is controversial.

[4] Quoted from Hamlyn (1968).

strained by inclination, requires not only a power of motivation apart from inclination, but the recognition of *reasons* that do not depend on inclination in any way.[5]

In the end, we will be interested in practical thought in general, where this includes not only acting on the basis of reasons, but also deliberation as an intentional action, being moved by reasons even when one does not act on them, and the forming and revising of intentions and desires. Does practical thought take place under the guise of the good? Is it best conceived as reflection about reasons, as such? I will argue that it is not, at least not in general. The details will have to wait for Part Two; but it is obvious that the treatment of intentional action will bear on them. Acting for reasons is the aspect of practical thought most commonly, and most plausibly, said to take place under the guise of the good.

In what follows, I make two arguments against this claim. The first is quite familiar: there seem to be cases of clear-eyed *akrasia*, and also of blindly unreflective action, in which we do things for reasons we do not see as good. Such examples have been discussed by Michael Stocker, in an important paper, and by others, too.[6] I will try to present them in a slightly more systematic way. But, in the end, this kind of argument is likely to lead to stalemate. So while I find it compelling, I also find it unsatisfying. This is what prompts the argument that occupies most of Part One. Instead of proceeding from the top down, from descriptions of cases to the nature of action, I argue from the bottom up. I begin with general constraints on a theory of intentional action, and show how these constraints rule out a normative interpretation of the recognition and adoption of reasons involved in acting on them. It is a central feature of my account that I do not deny that acting for reasons is acting reflectively, in a sense: it is acting *reflexively* in that it requires one to take an attitude to one's reasons for acting. But the attitude does not involve the belief that one's reasons are any good.

The structure of Part One is as follows. In section 1, I explain the puzzle about acting for reasons that motivates the rest of the discussion. In outline, the question is why two marks of intentional action go together: its susceptibility to explanation in terms of reasons, and its being subject to what Anscombe has called "knowledge without observation" (1963: 13–15). In particular, why should doing something for a reason require one

---

[5] On the connection between freedom and the moral law in Kant, see Allison (1986); the central passages appear in section III of the *Groundwork* (Kant 1785, 4: 446–7) and in the *Critique of Practical Reason* (Kant 1788, 5: 29). I criticize Kant's argument in Part Two, section 3.

[6] The paper is Stocker (1979). I have also been influenced, more diffusely, by the work of Harry Frankfurt.

to *believe* that one is doing it? This puzzle leads to some critical remarks about a simple belief-desire model of intentional action, which I reject in section 2. Its failure to solve the puzzle from section 1 goes along with another flaw: the belief-desire model leaves out the reflective nature of acting for reasons, the fact that we must *take* the reasons for which we act as reasons for acting as we do. This condition is what lends itself to normative interpretation, and thus to the guise of the good. Section 2 ends with a top-down argument against this claim, presenting cases in which we act for reasons without regarding our reasons for acting as good.

I argue, instead, that taking something as one's reason, in acting on it, is taking it as an *explanatory* reason, taking it to be a reason that explains one's action. There is nothing essentially normative about this: one need not take the reason to *justify* one's action in any way. I develop and defend this view in section 3, apply it to intentional action in general in section 4, and examine the extent to which it counts as a causal theory of action in section 5.

The upshot of these arguments is that reasons for acting must be seen as reasons, but need not be seen under the guise of good. In section 6, I elaborate on this result in two ways. I begin with some diagnostic remarks about the powerful appeal of the views that I reject. And I end with the obscure but popular claim that reasons-explanations make our actions "intelligible." Does this conflict with, and therefore undermine, the present account? Does it afford a plausible replacement for the guise of the good, on which explanations of action are ones "in which things are made intelligible by being revealed to be, or to approximate to being, as they rationally ought to be?"[7] I will argue that it does not: there is no reason to accept this normative conception of action-explanation, even if one agrees with Davidson and others about the constitutive role of rationality in psychological facts.

1. A Puzzle about *Intention*

In the course of a typical day, I do a multitude of things: I breathe almost continuously; I blink from time to time; I look at things, pick them up, and put them down; I eat and drink; I read; I listen to music; and I forget something I meant to bring to the office. All of this counts as my behaviour—what I *do* in a minimal sense—but not all of it is done intentionally. I *could* breathe and blink intentionally, but mostly I do not. My reading is almost always intentional—though I do read unintentionally from time to time, as for instance with the adverts on the side of a bus as I cross the

---

[7] The phrase is taken from McDowell (1985: 328).

street. And I never intentionally forget the things I need for my day of work. In what follows, I take for granted the idea of *doing* something, and ask what it is to do something *intentionally*.[8]

The focus on intentional action follows from our interest in the guise of the good. This is a doctrine about acting for reasons, and when we act for reasons, we always count as acting intentionally. The converse implication is less clear. According to Anscombe, an instance of action is intentional if and only if it is one "to which a certain sense of the question 'Why?' is given application; the sense is of course that in which the answer, if positive, gives a reason for acting" (1963: 9). But this question "is not refused application because the answer to it says that there is *no* reason" (1963: 25). Davidson denies the latter possibility: to act intentionally just *is* to act for reasons (Davidson 1963: 6). I return to this topic in section 4, where I argue that Anscombe is right: it is possible to act intentionally for no particular reason. What we need at present, however, is the claim on which Anscombe and Davidson agree: in acting for a reason, one must be acting intentionally.

So far, so good. The connection between reasons and intentional action, at least in this direction, is one that everyone accepts. Much of Anscombe's *Intention* is devoted to a more surprising claim: she argues that intentional action is subject to "knowledge without observation" (1963: 13–15). When an agent φs intentionally, he *knows* that he is φ-ing, and he knows this spontaneously, in a way that does not turn on observational evidence. More carefully, to know that *p* "without observation" is to have knowledge that is absolutely non-inferential: it does not depend on an inference from observation or any other kind of evidence, not even the vestigial inference that takes us from how things appear to a belief about how they are. (The exclusion of appearance is, I take it, one point of Anscombe 1963: 49–50.) In this respect, Anscombe compares the knowledge in intentional action to bodily awareness based on proprioception.

There are numerous difficulties here, both in Anscombe's account of bodily awareness, and in her attempt to contrast this knowledge, as "contemplative" or "speculative," with the "practical knowledge" involved in action (1963: 56–7). I want to concentrate, at first, on a simpler claim. Set

---

[8] So, our question is roughly, "What is left over if I subtract the fact that I raise my arm from the fact that I raise my arm intentionally?"—not Wittgenstein's (1953, §621) question, "What is left over if I subtract the fact that my arm goes up from the fact that I raise my arm?" I say that this is "roughly" our question, because it wrongly suggests that intentionality is always attached to an action that can also be performed unintentionally, one that it makes sense to consider with intentionality "subtracted." As I observe in section 5, following Anscombe (1963), this is not the case. Thus the question would be better put by asking, "What do intentional actions have in common in virtue of which they are intentional?"

aside the practical dimension of the knowledge that Anscombe describes. (That will be taken up in section 3.) Set aside, too, its allegedly non-inferential character. The basic insight of Anscombe's argument is that the "why?"-question, understood as a request for reasons, is "refused application by the answer: 'I was not aware that I was doing that'" (1963: 11). What I do unknowingly, I cannot do intentionally. More modestly, still— setting aside the claim to knowledge as well as the claim to knowledge without observation   I can only do intentionally what I *think* I am doing. Thus, for instance, if I have no idea that in humming Beethoven's Ninth I am driving my wife crazy, I simply cannot be driving her crazy *intentionally*—at least not so far as my humming goes. And if I am ignorant of the impatient tapping of my foot, as I pore over a draft of these pages, it too must be unintentional. It is important to stress that Anscombe's doctrine does not require *conscious* belief or awareness. I may believe that I am connecting an electrical circuit, and do so intentionally, as I turn on the light, without consciously reflecting on that fact. Once this is clear, it is tempting to say that one *cannot* do something intentionally in ignorance: without the belief that one is doing it.

There are exceptions to this rule, but they serve only to confirm the basic insight. Davidson famously considered one such case: "A man may be making ten carbon copies as he writes, and this may be intentional; yet he may not know that he is; all he knows is that he is trying" (1971: 50; see also 1978: 91–4). This example shows that Anscombe's doctrine is false, at least when it is unqualified. I can make ten carbon copies intentionally without having the belief, let alone knowledge, that I am doing so—it may seem to me quite doubtful that, even if I press as hard as I can, the copy will go through so many times. But the challenge to Anscombe is limited; even Davidson concedes that, when an agent acts intentionally, what he does "is known to him under *some* description" (1971: 50, my emphasis).

I think we can be more precise. When an agent φs intentionally without the belief that he is φ-ing, he is always doing something with the *end* of doing φ, where this something is an instance of intentional action in the paradigm sense that does involve belief, and where it is not just "trying to φ." Despite what Davidson suggests, it is not enough that the carbon-copier is intentionally *trying* to make ten copies, in the paradigm sense of "intentional action" that involves belief. He is and must be doing specific things—for instance, pressing hard on the paper—in that paradigm sense. This allows us to preserve a version of Anscombe's doctrine: when an agent acts intentionally, he must be doing something of which he has "practical knowledge"; or, to continue with our modesty about the claim to knowledge:

Belief: When someone is acting intentionally, there must be something he is doing intentionally, not merely trying to do, in the belief that he is doing it.

The central puzzles of action theory revolve around the truth of *Belief*. One puzzle is epistemic: what kind of warrant does one have for the beliefs that figure in intentional action? How are such beliefs justified? Pressing though it is, the epistemology of practical knowledge will not be a topic of this book. Even if I had a solution to its problems, they would take us too far afield. Instead we are concerned with a second great puzzle of action theory, a question raised, but never addressed, by Anscombe's *Intention*: what is the *connection* between the two marks of intentional action? More carefully, why should action done for reasons, or to which a certain sense of the question "why?" is given application, necessarily satisfy *Belief*? What is it about being-done-for-reasons—or being susceptible to the question "why?"—that requires the presence of belief?

The force of this question may be obscured in three ways. First, there is a tendency to focus on epistemic anxieties, in which we grant the presence of belief in intentional action, and question its claim to count as knowledge. This can lead us to miss the peculiarity of *Belief* itself. Second, we may suppose that Anscombe meets the challenge in her constructive account of answers to the question "why?" (1963: 24–5). But what she provides is not an account of *when* the question applies—one that entails *Belief*—but clarification of the question itself. Having identified the relevant sense of "why?" Anscombe offers no general theory of the conditions for its application, so the requirement of knowledge without observation (or mere belief) is never explained.

Finally, we may be misled by Anscombe's habitual appeal to public linguistic behaviour. She tends to think of the "why?"-question as something addressed to, and answered by, the agent herself. This is especially clear in her anxieties about whether the agent's answers will be *honest* (1963: 42–4, 48); and it is what leads her to reject the possibility that an agent might discover his reasons in psychoanalysis (1963: 26). If we think of the application of the "why?"-question as a matter of the answers an agent is disposed to give, it may seem to follow that it is "refused application" when the agent is not aware of what she is doing—for then she won't be disposed to give any reason for doing it, any more than she is disposed to offer an explanation of *any* fact of which she is unaware. But this argument trades on an ambiguity in Anscombe's criterion, one that is masked by her behaviourism. What is clear is that intentional action is that to which the question "why?" *has* application, understood as a request for reasons. The possibility of explanation by reasons is distinctive of intentional action. It is a further question whether, and why, the question has application only when the agent "gives it application" because she is able to answer it. In particular, why must she have a true belief about what she is doing, in order to be doing it for reasons at all? Why isn't it sufficient for reasons-explanation that she knows what she *intends* to do, or what she is *trying* to do?[9] More strongly, why must she have any belief about what she is up to, at all? Why is it not enough for her action to be motivated by the right desire?

In effect, the puzzle about *Intention* is to explain the necessary connection between acting for reasons and having a true belief about what one is doing. It may seem odd to demand an explanation for a necessary truth. But the demand is quite familiar, even if this way of putting it is not. We are faced with two marks of intentional action: its connection with reasons, and its connection with belief. The question is why something that satisfies the first mark of intentional action must satisfy the second. A necessary truth cannot be mere happenstance, so there must be something in the nature of intentional action, something in *what it is* to be done for reasons—or to be susceptible to a certain sense of the question "why?"—that requires the presence of belief.[10] To give a plausible account of this connection is a condition of adequacy on a philosophical theory of acting for reasons. An account of what it is to be done for reasons, or to be susceptible to Anscombe's sense of the question "why?"

---

[9] On some accounts of intentional action, it *is* enough for the agent to believe that she intends to do something, or that she is trying to do it, so that *Belief* is false. (Compare Falvey 2001: 21 on the "two-factor thesis.") This sort of view is typically motivated by anxieties about the epistemic status of the beliefs involved in intentional action. Anscombe argues conclusively against some attempts to "push what is known [in intentional action] back and back; first to bodily movement, then perhaps to the contraction of the muscles, then to the attempt to do the thing, which comes right at the beginning." Her point is that "[the] only description that I clearly know of what I am doing may be of something that is at a distance from me" (Anscombe 1963: 53). A complete treatment of doubts about *Belief* would have to undermine the epistemic anxieties that motivate them. I won't attempt that here, for two reasons. First, I think it is clear that, apart from epistemic doubts, the phenomenology of intentional action unequivocally supports *Belief*, and thus generates the puzzle I am pressing in the main text. Second, the puzzle would survive the proposed revision of *Belief*, applied now to the need for beliefs about one's intentions, or what one is *trying* to do, if not about what one is actually doing. The real puzzle is about the need for *cognition* of one's action, in acting for reasons, however mediated it may be.

[10] I mean to be appealing, here, to an intuitive style of argument, presented more explicitly than is usual. The demand to *explain* a necessary truth, or to make it un-mysterious, is increasingly common in discussions of *supervenience*; see, for instance, Blackburn (1993: 145). And it figures often in debates about the adequacy of a "philosophical account" of some contested subject-matter: a good account of *what X is* ought to accommodate—that is, entail, and thus explain—its necessary connections with Y and Z. The principles behind these arguments have been explored by Fine (1994), who wants to explain necessity in terms of *essence*, and by Dorr (2004, sections 1 and 3). But the general idea is relatively noncommittal: we have to account for necessary connections by appeal to the natures of the things that they connect.

should entail the necessity of *Belief*. To articulate and defend such an account is a task for a theory of intentional action. Why is it that, when an agent acts for reasons, there must be something she does in the *belief* that she is doing it?[11]

Even before we explore the implications of this puzzle for the guise of the good, we should note a significant consequence. It follows from the need to explain *Belief* that we cannot take acting for a reason as *basic* or *primitive*.[12] When A is doing φ because *p*, she is acting intentionally, and so she must be doing something in the belief that she is doing it. In order to account for this necessity, we need to break down what is involved in acting for a reason; we need to see how one of its elements is, or involves, the relevant belief. This is one source of pressure towards reductive psychological accounts of acting for reasons, and of intentional action in general—accounts that appeal to the causal-motivational role of the agent's beliefs and desires. If we cannot take the "because" of reasons-explanation as primitive, and if our account is required to entail *Belief*, it is natural to begin with the idea that acting for a reason can be explained in terms of the agent's psychological states. In the next section, I turn to a simple belief-desire model of intentional action. The defects of this model will lead us to the guise of the good, and its defects, in turn, will point towards a solution to the puzzle about *Belief*.

2. THE BELIEF-DESIRE MODEL

Reasons for acting, in one sense, are considerations that count in favour of doing something. To say that there is a reason for me to finish this book is to point to a justification for doing so. In saying what the reason is, we specify the content of the justification. It is reasons, in this sense—*good*

---

[11] Readers familiar with *Practical Reflection* (Velleman 1989) may wonder how this question relates to the one that Velleman asks at the beginning of his book. If I understand him correctly, Velleman's question cannot be the one that I am asking here. Although he wants to "explain why, in the normal case, you already know what you're doing, or at least what you're trying to do, without ever finding out," Velleman (1989: 26) does not purport to explain the *necessity* of *Belief*. What he provides is a *hypothetical model* of rational agency on which belief is involved in intentional action (Velleman 1989: 5–8). He argues that creatures who desire self-knowledge would be capable of acting for reasons, and that, in doing so, they would know what they were doing. But he takes it to be an empirical question not only "[w]hether human beings are [. . .] rational agents" but "how rational agency is realized in them" (Velleman 1989: 5). He does not attempt to show that rational agency *must* be realized in a way that vindicates *Belief*, or to derive *Belief* from the very idea of intentional action. In this respect, the explanatory project I take up here is more ambitious than the explanatory project of Velleman's book.

[12] For this suggestion, see Dancy (2000: 161–3), responding to Davidson (1963: 9–11).

reasons or *normative* reasons—that are conceptually related to the conditions of good practical thought.[13]

It is an unfortunate fact that we do not always act for good reasons. We may not be aware of the considerations that count as reasons in our circumstance. We may be aware of them, and yet unmoved. And we may be moved to act by considerations that are *not* good reasons; and by ones that are not even facts. In asking about someone's reason for acting on a given occasion, we are asking about something that *might* be a good reason—or not.

It is clear, then, that the canonical expression of an agent's reason,

A did ϕ for the reason that *p*

does not entail that the fact that *p* was a *good* reason for A to ϕ. (This is true even if reasons must be seen under the guise of the good: when we take our reasons to justify our action, to some degree, we may be making a mistake.) It is less well-known, but just as clear, that the agent's reason need not be a fact. In *Practical Reality*, Jonathan Dancy gives examples of this (2000: 132):

> His reason for doing it was that it would increase his pension, but in fact he was quite wrong about that.

> The ground on which he acted was that she had lied to him, though actually she had done nothing of the sort.

There are complications here. For instance, things may be different with "A did ϕ *because p*," when this is used to give an agent's reason. Here there is pressure to read the claim as factive, and even to suppose that it entails "A knew that *p*."[14] It is not clear to me that this is right. I suspect that "because" can be used to *mean* "for the reason that," where it is clear that the latter idiom is not factive. But nothing turns on such subtleties of usage. For my purposes, all that matters is that the second canonical expression of an agent's reason,

A did ϕ because *p*

entails the first, and does not entail that the fact that *p* is a *good* reason to act.

The idea of an agent's reason has led to much confusion, some of which is merely terminological. As Dancy (2000: 112–20) insists, what we substitute for the schematic letter "*p*" in our expression of an agent's reason

---

[13] See the introduction, section 1.

[14] Hyman (1999: 441–2) insists on this, but goes too far in suggesting that "A did ϕ for the reason that *p*" entails "A knew that *p*." The connection with knowledge, if it exists at all, is confined to the use of "because" in giving an agent's reason.

is something that refers to a *consideration*, a putative fact, a candidate to be a good reason. In this sense, an agent's reasons are *not* a matter of his psychological states—except in odd cases, where his psychology has to be taken into account in his deliberation. (In Dancy's example—from Dancy 2000: 125—"[someone] who believes that there are pink rats living in his shoes may take that he believes this as a reason to go to the doctor or perhaps a psychoanalyst.") Even if acting for reasons is to be understood in terms of the causal role of psychological states, it would be a mistake to describe these states as "the agent's reasons." The mistake I am warning against can be encouraged by the use of "motivating reason" to refer to the psychological states that motivate action, and by Davidson's (1963: 3–4) idea of a *"primary reason."*[15] It is crucial to see that "motivating reason" and "primary reason" are terms of art; they do not correspond to the ordinary use of "reason" in speaking of *good* reasons, which are facts, *or* its use in giving an *agent's* reasons, which are putative facts. Nothing but muddle can result from being careless about this.

That being so, the best way to think about the belief-desire model of acting for reasons is not as the claim that our reasons for acting are really beliefs and desires, but as an attempt to say what it is to act for a reason (where the reason is a putative fact) in causal-psychological terms. It is, in effect, a reductive metaphysical account of "acting because *p*" or "acting for the reason that *p*"—not a rejection of that common-sense idiom. Those who think that acting for a reason is a matter of motivation by belief and desire can agree that it is possible literally to act for good reasons: a normative reason is precisely the sort of thing that can *be* a reason for which one acts.[16] It follows that, even on the belief-desire model, the ambiguity of "reason" is not like the ambiguity of "bank." The senses of "reason"—normative and explanatory—are closely related. A normative or *good* reason is, so to speak, a good thing to have as one's reason: it is

---

[15] For the idiom of "motivating reasons" see, especially, Smith (1987; 1994).

[16] I think this point is missed by Dancy (2000: 98–107), in his critique of "psychologism." He assumes that, for the psychological theorist, the "because" of "A did φ because *p*" must be a matter of efficient causation. This would force a revisionary account, at least in the case in which it is false that *p*, since causal explanation is factive. Even when it is true that *p*, Dancy thinks that the psychological account must adopt a "three-part story" in which the fact that *p* causes the belief that *p*, and the belief then causes what the agent does. See Dancy (2000: 101, 105–6); Smith (1998: 157, 175). Thus, it may seem, the psychological theorist cannot take "A did φ because *p*" at face value; it can only be a crude way of speaking, something to be replaced in a philosophically perspicuous account of action. If this is Dancy's argument, however, it rests on a mistake. For it is no part of a sensible psychologism that the "because" of "A did φ because *p*" is that of efficient causation. The point is precisely to explain one sort of "because"—the "because" of agents' reasons—in terms of *another*: the "because" of (causal) motivation. Dancy's mistake is to think that "because" must be univocal in the explanation of action; and that is something the sensible psychologist denies.

a fact that corresponds, in accordance with *Reasons*, to a good disposition of practical thought.[17]

The belief-desire model derives mainly from the work of Davidson, in the papers that appear as Part I of *Essays on Actions and Events* (1980)—though he is not clear as one might wish about the points made in the previous paragraph. A pared-down version of his approach, which Velleman calls "the standard model," explains the nature of intentional action as follows:

> We want something to happen, and we believe that some behavior of ours would constitute or produce or at least promote its happening. These two attitudes jointly cause the relevant behaviour, and in doing so they manifest the causal powers that are partly constitutive of their being, respectively, a desire and a belief. Because these attitudes also justify the behavior that they cause, that behavior eventuates not only *from causes* but *for reasons*. (Velleman 2000b: 5)

In general, acting because p is being motivated to act by the belief that p, together with an appropriate accompanying desire. The project of this section is to explore the prospects for this belief-desire account.

Before I turn to the explanation of *Belief*, it is a worth taking a moment to address the most common objection to the claim that acting for a reason, or intentional action in general, can be explained in causal-motivational terms. (This is not a digression: the concept of motivation is one that I employ in giving my own account.) The problem arises from the fact that motivation by belief and desire is a matter of efficient causation—but not just any causal process will do. There are cases of "wayward" or "deviant" causation by our psychological states, which evidently do not suffice for intentional action. In Davidson's well-known example, a nervous climber wants to be rid of his companion's dangerous weight, and knows that he can manage this by dropping his rope; he becomes increasingly anxious as a result, and this prompts him, carelessly, to let go (1973: 79). His action of letting go is caused by the right sort of belief and desire, according to the standard model, but not in the right way. He does not drop his partner's rope intentionally.

In his discussion of this case, Davidson concludes that we cannot give an illuminating explanation of "causal deviance." We have to take it as basic. But that would make the connection between causation and motivation a mystery—the same kind of mystery as the puzzle about *Belief*.

---

[17] The principle of *Reasons* was explained, and argued for, in the introduction:

> *Reasons*: The fact that p is a reason for A to ϕ just in case A has a collection of psychological states, C, such that the disposition to be moved to ϕ by C-and-the-belief-that-p is a good disposition of practical thought, and C contains no false beliefs.

(Why does motivation imply causation? What is the connection between the two?) It is essential to the belief-desire approach to solve the problem of causal deviance, at least in outline.

And, in fact, I think the problem *can* be solved. Following Davidson (1973: 78–9), we should distinguish deviance in the causation of basic action from deviance in the causation of non-basic action—action that an agent performs by doing something else intentionally, with that end. In the case of basic action, the crucial concept is that of *guidance*: when an agent φs intentionally, he *wants* to φ, and this desire not only causes but continues to guide behaviour towards its object.[18] (It is this condition that fails in Davidson's example.) Sustained causation of a process towards a goal is not unique to intentional action: it is present in purposive behaviour that is not intentional. So although it is something of which we lack an adequate theory, there is no circularity in taking it for granted here.[19] The motivation of non-basic action is to be explained in terms of its relationship with the basic actions by which it is performed. If I do something with the end of doing φ, I must have a plan for doing φ by performing that action, and I count as doing φ intentionally just in case I do it in accordance with my plan. (I say more about acting with a further end, and about the motivation of non-basic action, at the end of section 4.) Finally, there is the possibility of causal deviance not only in the motivation of action, but of intention and desire. Here I think the problem is less severe: the "right way" depends upon the dispositions of the agent. The causing of one mental state by another is non-deviant, in A, just in case A is *disposed* to make this transition, and this disposition was operative in its taking place. In effect, the disposition ensures that the causal transition is no accident; it is part of the ordinary course of A's mental life.[20]

If this sketch is basically right, the belief-desire account can solve the problem of causal deviance. What it cannot solve is the puzzle about *Be-*

[18] The claim that desire is always involved in the motivation of intentional action does not amount to the "Humean theory of motivation," since it allows for the desire itself to be motivated by belief (Nagel 1970: 29–30). That desire is involved in the proximate motivation of intentional action is, or ought to be, common ground between "Humeans" like Smith (1987) and their anti-Humean opponents. I discuss the Humean theory in Part Two, section 4.

[19] In appealing to the idea of "guidance" by desire, or towards a goal, I follow Frankfurt (1978). His discussion is framed as an *attack* on causal theories of action, including Davidson's (see Frankfurt 1978: 70, n. 1), but it is really directed against an appeal to "prior causal history," instead of the causal process involved in action, as it occurs. (I return to this point in section 5.) For steps towards a theory of causal guidance in purposive behaviour, see Juarrero (1999).

[20] I return to this point about dispositions, and deal with an objection, at the end of section 6.

lief. On the standard model, intentional action is motivated by a desire and a belief about how to achieve the object of that desire. (In the limiting case, of *basic* action, the belief drops out.) But an agent can be motivated by the desire for an end, and the belief that doing φ is a more or less effective means to that end, without having the belief that he is doing φ. The presence of that belief does not follow from belief-desire motivation; nor does it follow that there is *anything* he does in the belief that he is doing it. If the standard model were correct, *Belief* would not be a necessary truth. But it is; and so the standard model is false.[21]

This argument demonstrates the force of the explanatory demand derived in section 1: the need to account for *Belief.* It shows that this demand has bite. Although it seems to call for a psychological account of acting for reasons, it is not satisfied by a simple appeal to motivation by belief and desire. That would make *Belief* mysterious. Something is missing from the standard model. But what?

One way to diagnose the failure of the standard model is to look at the sort of cases in which it goes awry. As Velleman (2000b: 2–9) has shown, there are occasions on which our behaviour is guided purposively by desire, but on which it seems quite wrong to say that we are acting for reasons. His examples draw on Freudian themes. In one narrative, Freud's sister tells him that his attractive new desk is marred only by his old inkstand, which does not match. Later, Freud sweeps the inkstand on to the floor, with a peculiar and remarkable clumsiness (Velleman 2000b: 2–3). On Freud's interpretation, and Velleman's, Freud is moved to break the inkstand by the belief that breaking it will persuade his sister to buy him a new one, and the desire for a matching inkstand. His behaviour meets the conditions of the standard model. It is caused by the desire for an end, and a belief about how to achieve that end. And this causation is nondeviant, since the desire to break the inkstand guides the movements of Freud's arm in sweeping it to the floor. Despite all this, Freud did not act *intentionally* in breaking the inkstand, and he did not break it for a *rea-*

---

[21] In addressing this argument to Davidson's theory of intentional action, we have to deal with a complication. His view is that, "[whenever] someone does something for a reason [. . .] he can be characterized as (*a*) having some sort of pro attitude towards actions of a certain kind, and (*b*) *believing (or knowing, perceiving, noticing, remembering) that his action is of that kind*" (Davidson 1963: 3–4, my emphasis). The second clause has two interpretations. If it merely requires one to believe that a certain action *would* belong to the desired kind (as in Velleman's "standard model"), it does not entail *Belief.* If it requires one to believe that one is *performing* an action of the desired kind, it does entail *Belief*—but we need to know *why* the first interpretation is not enough. Why does it take more to attach one's reason to one's action than motivation by belief? This question points in the direction of the remarks that follow in the main text, about *taking* something as one's reason to act.

son. Although it would be right to say that Freud knocked the inkstand with his arm out of a desire to break it, it would be wrong to say that he did so *in order to* break it, or on the *ground* that doing so would break it. There seem to be two levels of explanation here: one of mere psychological motivation, which does apply to Freud, and one of acting on the basis of a reason, which does not.

Freud's case is peculiar in several ways. For one thing, it does not involve knowledge without observation or spontaneous belief. For another thing, it seems to matter that Freud did not *decide* upon his actions and did not *intend* to perform them. Intention is missing from the standard model.[22] It is not clear how much we learn from this. *Why* must an agent who does ϕ because *p* intend to be doing ϕ? What *is* an intention to act? But there may be progress of a sort. For it is a familiar, if controversial, claim about intention that it requires *belief*: an agent who intends to ϕ must believe that she is going to ϕ.[23] The most powerful argument for this claim is due to Anscombe: the verbal expression of the intention to ϕ is the assertoric utterance of the sentence "I am going to ϕ" (see Anscombe 1963: 1), and thus the expression of *belief* that one is going to ϕ. Anscombe is writing about *prospective* intention, or intention for the future, not "[one's] intention *in* doing or proposing something" (1963: 1), what one intends to be doing now. But a similar point applies to intentions of the latter kind: the verbal expression of the intention to be doing ϕ is the assertion that one is doing it. If we could account for this fact, and for the fact that acting for reasons requires intention, to the extent that it does, we would have the basis for an illuminating explanation of *Belief*.

Despite its appeal, I won't pursue this path below. This is in part because I do not want to rely on the claim that intention requires belief—that will be a consequence, not an assumption, of the arguments to come. (I return to it in section 4.) And it is in part because there are cases of motivation by belief that do not count as acting for a reason, even though

---

[22] It is also missing from Davidson's account, as he later came to see (Davidson 1963: 7–8; 1978: 83–6). The absence of intention marks a difference between the "standard model" discussed in the introduction to Velleman (2000b), and in the text above, and the "standard story" rejected by Velleman (1992b)—despite his claim that these discussions deal with the same phenomenon (Velleman 2000b: 2, n. 3). In the earlier paper, the story of action *does* include the forming of an intention to act, and I think it therefore succeeds in giving a sufficient condition for intentional action. Velleman (1992b) may be right that this more sophisticated view still cannot account for the robust involvement of the agent—as in "autonomous" or "wholehearted" action, perhaps—but this is something that goes beyond our question about acting for reasons.

[23] For this doctrine, see, especially, Hampshire and Hart (1958), Harman (1976), and Velleman (1989, ch. 4). Critics of the doctrine include Davidson (1978: 91–4), Bratman (1981: 254–6; 1984: 384–5) and Mele (1992, ch. 8).

they do involve the intention to act. Suppose that I am convinced that I ought to be a lawyer, but only because I was pressured into it by my parents. As I go through law school, I truly believe that I am suited to this kind of work. I do not respond to the clues that indicate otherwise: the fact that I spend much less time working than my peers; that I often feel tired and lethargic; that I never get very good grades. I would never act on these reasons, as grounds on which to quit. Still I might *decide* to quit, and be moved to do so, unconsciously, by beliefs that correspond to these facts—finding my own decision both capricious and hard to explain.[24] Again there seem to be two levels of explanation here: one of mere psychological motivation, which does apply to me, and one of acting on the basis of a reason, which does not. I do not quit *in order to* find a more appropriate career, or on the *ground* that I am not enjoying law school, even though I am moved by the corresponding beliefs. We must not be misled, in such a case, by the use of "reason" to mean no more than "cause." We can speak of the fact that I wasn't suited to being a lawyer as the reason why I left law school, just as we speak of the fact that the wind was strong as the reason why the bridge collapsed. In neither case is the reason acted on by the "agent" involved; it is simply an efficient cause.

Our question, then, is what makes for the difference between the two levels of explanation. What is involved in acting for a reason beyond the kind of motivation described by the standard model? Perhaps the most influential view, and in some ways the most obvious, is that, in our examples of defective agency, the agent does not *see* the considerations by which he is moved *as* good reasons to act. What is missing from the standard model, on this response, is the doctrine of the guise of the good. This is how Velleman reacts to his story from Freud:

> A reason for acting is something that warrants or justifies behaviour. In order to serve as the basis for a subject's behaviour, it must justify that behaviour to the subject—that is, in his eyes—and it must thereby engage some rational disposition of his to do what's justified, to behave in accordance with justifications. (Velleman 2000b: 9)

The same suggestion is Joseph Raz, who describes it as the "classical approach" to intentional action, and traces it to Plato and Aristotle, through

---

[24] A similar story is told by Nomy Arpaly, though she regards it as a genuine case of acting for a reason (2003: 50–1). Her argument for this description is weak. According to Arpaly, "[the] root of the feeling that [such characters] cannot be acting for reasons seems to lie in the fact that they do not *deliberate* upon these reasons, and their ultimate actions are not the result of deliberation" (2003: 51). That is not the case. Even those who agree that acting for a reason does not require explicit deliberation can see the contrast between mere psychological motivation and acting on a reason, as such. The arguments in the main text attempt to characterize what is missing here, without appeal to an excessively reflective or self-conscious conception of intentional action.

Anscombe's *Intention* (Raz 1999: 22–3). In an earlier paper, Raz puts the point as follows:

> Both choice and decision are subject to rules of rational constraint, the most important of which is that one can only choose or decide for a reason, *i.e. for what one takes to be a good reason for the option chosen.* Even irrational choice is choice for a reason [in this sense]. (1997: 8, my emphasis)

As I said in the introduction, this kind of view is very widely held.[25] Part of its appeal is that it adds to the standard model in a way that might explain what is missing from the cases discussed above. So, for instance, I do not accept there is *good reason* for me to drop out of law school, even as I decide to do so. And while Freud may believe that he has a justification for breaking the inkstand, this belief is not involved in the behaviour by which he does it. When he knocks the inkstand to the floor, his desire is acting through him, without his warrant.

There is something deeply right about this. To act for reasons is to base one's action on reasons, as such. When I decide to go for a walk because the weather is fine, I *take* that fact about the weather *as* my reason to act. This seems to be in part a volitional and in part a cognitive matter: I adopt a consideration as my reason, and thereby regard it as such. It is in this intuitive conception of acting for reasons that we must find the seeds of an adequate theory.

It is clear that this will take some digging around: the rhetoric of "taking as a reason" needs to be explained. What is the peculiar attitude we have towards our reasons when we act on them? But even before we see the details, there is reason to doubt the common view—expressed in the quotations above—that taking something as one's reason involves the belief that it is a good reason on which to act. The most compelling examples, here, are ones in which our desires are out of line with what we value, or think worthwhile. In a particularly vivid description of this, Watson imagines someone who thinks that sexual desire is the work of the devil; "the man who is estranged from his sexual inclinations does not acknowledge even a prima facie reason for sexual activity; that he is sexually inclined towards certain activities is not even *a* consideration" (1975: 210). Still, we might add, he can certainly *act* on such a desire, and act intentionally—without regarding the reason for which he is acting

---

[25] Note, however, that in the passage cited here, Raz is making two distinct claims: first, that intentional action (he talks about "choice") is always done for reasons, and second, that reasons for acting must be seen under the guise of the good. The first claim sides with Davidson over Anscombe on acting "for no particular reason," and I come back to it in section 4. It is the second claim that is our main concern. Versions of this claim are found in Anscombe (1963: 21–5), Milligan (1974: 183), Darwall (1983: 205), Bond (1983: 30–1), Walker (1989: 670), Broome (1997), Korsgaard (1997: 221), Wallace (1999), and Velleman (1992a: 101; 1992b: 140–2), among others.

(to satisfy his sexual urge) as any good. Or consider, instead, someone who enjoys philosophy for the sense of power it can give, even though he does not see such pleasures as worthwhile in the least.[26] He asks derisive questions at talks because that will humiliate the visiting speaker. This is his reason for acting—he does so intentionally—but he recognizes all the while that it is not a good reason to act. (It is tempting to imagine that he must despise himself for this behaviour; but he may not.) It seems to me simply naïve to insist, in such a case, that the agent must see something good in what he is doing, some justification for his behaviour. On the contrary, it is just what he feels like doing.[27] More generally, while there are cases of *akrasia* in which one sees some reason to act against one's better judgement, there are also cases in which one sees no reason at all. When I decide to smoke an entire pack of cigarettes tonight because I won't be able to do so tomorrow, having quit at midnight, I know that this fact does nothing to justify my action. It says nothing in favour of smoking the cigarettes, which I will not even enjoy. Even as I act for this reason, I know that I am irrational in giving it any weight at all.

A final example, which turns on a curious mistake in Anscombe's *Intention*. Suppose that, as in a well-known paper by Warren Quinn (1993), I find myself with a brute inclination to turn on radios, not in order to hear music or get the news, or for any further reason. In acting on this inclination—for instance, in deciding to turn on the radio in my office— I may well be acting intentionally.[28] But I do not see anything good or worthwhile in having the radio on. Now this is not, so far, a clear example of acting for a *reason* I do not see as good, for it may be said that I turn on the radio "for no particular reason." That would be Anscombe's response:

> Aristotle would seem to have held that every action done by a rational agent was capable of having its grounds set forth up to a premise containing a desirability characterization; and as we have seen, there is a reasonable ground for this view, wherever there is calculation of means to ends, or of ways of doing

---

[26] This case is adapted from a striking passage in Burnyeat (1980: 76).

[27] On desiring the bad, or the indifferent, see Stocker (1979) and Velleman (1992a). Velleman's discussion is perplexing. He argues convincingly that someone can act for reasons without seeing anything good in what he is doing. But he insists that "I cannot act for reasons if I don't care about doing what's justified or (as I would prefer to put it) what makes sense" (Velleman 1992a: 121). I don't see why not. According to Velleman, in acting from despair, "I am determined never to do a good or desirable or positive thing again." But surely I am also indifferent to whether my actions are justified, and I could not care less whether what I am doing makes sense.

[28] Quinn says that my disposition does not "rationalize" my turning on the radio; but he means that it does not make it "(even *prima facie*) rational" to do so; "my odd pro-attitude gives me no reason to turn on radios" (Quinn 1993: 236–7). He does not deny that my disposition could *motivate* a fully intentional act.

what one wants to do. [. . .] Aristotle's specifications for the action of a rational agent do not cover the case of 'I just did, for no particular reason'. (Anscombe 1963: 72–3)

The problem is that, once we admit the possibility of acting intentionally
for no particular reason, we *have* to admit the possibility of acting for a
reason one does not see as good. Suppose, for instance, that I plug in my
office radio *because* I am going to turn it on. Here I do something for a
reason, but since I see nothing good or worthwhile in turning the radio
on—I am acting from a brute inclination—I can hardly see the fact that I
am doing so as a *good reason* to take the necessary means. It follows that
Anscombe is wrong to insist that practical reasoning, when it is a matter
of calculating how to achieve one's ends, always begins with a desire that
depicts its object "under the aspect of some good" (1963: 75; see also
1989: 31–4).

I find these arguments against the guise of the good, applied to reasons
for acting, entirely convincing. Whatever it turns out to be, acting for a
reason does not require the belief that one's reason is good. The problem
is that my examples, and others like them, are not persuasive to everyone.
Devoted advocates of a normative conception of agency typically insist
that there *is* a sense in which the agents I have described regard their
actions as warranted—we just need a suitably weak conception of "reason" or "warrant." Or they deny that they are really cases of intentional
action: the nasty philosopher must be overcome by malice; his actions are
involuntary, and do not really belong to him. This sounds to me like special pleading. But I do not like the ensuing stalemate. And there is in any
case a defect in the argument from cases, even if it works: it prompts the
view that acting for reasons is acting under the guise of the good *for the
most part*, or when other things are equal. It depends on thoughts about
good reasons, except in the presence of emotional disturbance or mental
conflict. Isn't that enough?

In my view, even such qualified claims are false. It is not just that we can
act for reasons we regard as bad, as in some kinds of *akrasia*, or that
depression or apathy can make us indifferent to what we should do, but
that *in general* taking something as one's reason is not a matter of taking
it as good. Even fully rational agents, and fully virtuous ones, need not
believe in the *merit* of the reasons for which they act.[29] It is not just the
desperate, but also the unreflective and the unconcerned, who may not
bother with evaluative judgement. That will be a consequence of the arguments to come.

---

[29] Here I may depart somewhat from the lessons of Stocker (1979), whose examples of
acting *not* under the guise of the good depend on such things as spiritual failure, self-hatred,
and spite.

3. ACTING FOR REASONS

Let us take stock. We have seen that the guise of the good, for reasons, can be motivated by the defects of the standard belief-desire model of intentional action.[30] One defect of this model is that it does not explain *Belief*. A second defect is its failure to accommodate the *active* and *reflective* character of the attitude we take to reasons, in acting on them. Our reasons are in some sense "up to us"—we decide *why* to do something, as well as what to do—and we seem to recognize our reasons, as such. It was the second defect, about *taking* something as one's reason—and not the puzzle about *Belief*—that led us to the guise of the good.

Although the defects of the standard model are thus distinct, their remedies must be related. The explanation of *Belief* must lie in a correct account of taking-as-one's-reason. It will otherwise be possible to take something as one's reason, and act on that basis—thereby acting *for that reason*—without any belief about what one is doing. *Belief* would be have to be false. In what follows, I argue that this explanatory constraint conflicts with the common interpretation of taking-as-one's-reason in terms of the guise of the good.

What is involved in taking something as one's reason to act? The question can be broken down. What is the *attitude* we have to our reasons in acting on them? And what *content* does this attitude have? Let us begin with the attitude. It is no coincidence, I think, that we are inclined to speak of "taking" here. This suggests, at once, a *practical* meaning ("taking" as laying hold of, or making use of) and an *epistemic* one ("taking" as understanding, or taking to be the case). *Both* meanings are involved when we say that someone who acts because *p* takes *p* as his reason to act.[31] In doing so, he thinks of *p* as his reason to act, and he is moved by this recognition. Taking something as my reason is a kind of "desire-like belief." It is a belief-like representation of *p* as my reason to act, and at the same time a decision to act on that reason, something by which I am led to do so.

In saying this, I am trying to combine two insights. The first is that we *choose* the reasons on which we act. There are many reasons for which I might decide to write a book: personal satisfaction, a fragment of immortality, professional ambition. I am not passive in the face of this: even if I believe that books give their authors a kind of immortality, and even if I

---

[30] The arguments of this section revise and replace those that appear in the corresponding section ("What is Intentional Action?") of Setiya (2004b).

[31] Strictly speaking, the phrase "taking *p* as one's reason to act," should be "taking *the consideration that p* as one's reason to act," so that "*p*" can be read consistently as a schematic letter. I won't bother to be careful about this.

think that this is a reason—a good reason—to write a book, it may not be *my* reason for doing so. That is up to me. (Note that we can say this without begging the question against the guise of the good; it may still be true that the reason I choose must be one that I regard as good.) The second insight is that we know without observation not only *what* we are doing, but *why*. Just as I can only do intentionally what I think I am doing (with the proviso about Davidson's carbon-copier), I know what my *reasons* are without having to find out.[32] I don't have to ask myself why I am walking to the shops, if my reason for doing so is to buy a hammer. (If I do have to ask myself, and no answer can be found, my action has become detached from reasons; I am doing it aimlessly, if I am doing it intentionally at all.) The moral of these insights is the one implied by the two meanings of "take." Taking something as one's reason is both desiderative or motivational *and* cognitive. It is a matter of desire-like belief.

It is essential to contrast this picture of the attitude involved in acting for a reason with the "judgement internalism" on which there are propositions one cannot believe without being motivated in the appropriate way. It is sometimes held that this applies to the proposition that something is good, or to propositions about what there is reason to do. Whether or not that is the case, it is a radically different sort of claim from the one that I intend. My point is not that the belief involved in taking something as one's reason *entails* desire, but that taking-as-one's-reason is not simply belief, or desire, but a state that has features of both. Like belief, it represents its content as being true—after all, I know what my reasons are. And like desire, it has the power to cause or motivate the action it depicts, and to cause it to be done for the reason in question. I am not claiming that the second feature follows from the first. They are separate features, combined in the attitude of taking-as-one's-reason.

Some philosophers deny that this kind of combination is possible. In particular, Michael Smith has argued that nothing could have the "direction of fit" of belief and desire at once, at least not in relation to the same proposition (1987: 54–6). I respond to his argument near the beginning of section 4. For the moment, let us press on with the idea that taking-as-one's-reason is a matter of desire-like belief, hoping further to justify it by its consequences. What we need to investigate next is the *content* of this attitude, and its role in the explanation of *Belief*.

There is an obvious suggestion here, for those who defend the guise of the good: to take something as one's reason is to have the desire-like belief

---

[32] The same point is made by Audi (1986: 82–5), in a qualified form, and by Searle (2001: 16). See also Wallace (1999: 241). (Note, however, that Wallace accepts the normative interpretation of taking-as-one's-reason that I am in the midst of arguing against.)

that it is a *good* reason on which to act. This is what we must add to the belief-desire model, in order to deal with the cases (Freud and the reluctant lawyer) described in section 2. And, so its proponents say, it is the most natural and plausible account of what is involved in certifying something as one's reason to act. One takes it to *justify* what one is doing, at least to some extent; and that is part of why one is doing it.

Even apart from the examples at the end of section 2, however, this proposal is problematic: it makes a mystery of *Belief*. For it simply does not follow from the fact that I take *p* as a good reason to φ, and thus *believe* that it is a good reason to φ, that I believe that I am actually doing φ, or that I am doing anything at all. I can believe that there is good reason to do something without believing that I am doing it, or even trying to do it; there are lots of good reasons on which I do not act. If taking something as one's reason were taking it to be a good reason, one could act on that basis, and thus act for a reason, without any belief about what one is doing. *Belief* would turn out to be false.

Taking something as a *good* reason to act is therefore not sufficient for the attitude involved in acting on it. Nor can we simply *add* that, in taking something as one's reason for doing φ, one must take oneself to be doing it. That is what needs to be explained. Or, more carefully, we need to account for this:

> *Belief*: When someone is acting intentionally, there must be something he is doing intentionally, not merely trying to do, in the belief that he is doing it.

The guise of the good does nothing to help explain *why* action that is done for reasons, or intentional action in general, must satisfy *Belief*.

It does not follow from this alone that, in acting for reasons, we do not act under the guise of the good. But it gives that claim considerable force: the guise of the good gives the wrong interpretation of taking-as-one's-reason; and it does nothing to solve the puzzle about *Belief*. In order to *prove* that it is redundant we need to find a better theory of taking-as-one's-reason, one that entails *Belief* but does not support the guise of the good. The key to this theory is to recognize the ambiguity of "reason": the use that corresponds to practical justification, and the one that corresponds to Anscombe's sense of the question "why?"

Suppose that I am walking outside because the weather is fine. I take that fact about the weather as my reason for walking, and that is why I am doing so. On the normative interpretation, or the guise of the good, this means that I take the fact that the weather is fine as a *good* reason to walk outside. But that already sounds odd, for plain linguistic reasons. When I act because *p*, I take *p* as *my* reason to act, not just—or not even—as *a* reason to act. I take it as the reason for which I am acting, and I know without observation that it is. This suggests a frankly circular account of the attitude to reasons involved in acting on them:

> To take p as one's reason for doing ϕ is to have the desire-like belief that one is doing ϕ for the reason that p.

The sense of "reason" in which one takes something as one's reason is *explanatory*, not *justifying*. When I go for my walk because the weather is fine, I am motivated by a state that is at once the belief that I am walking outside for that reason, and like a desire in causing me to do it (and to do it for that reason).

Whatever its difficulties, this interpretation of taking-as-one's-reason would help to explain *Belief*. If I believe that I am doing ϕ for the reason that p, it follows trivially that I believe that I am doing ϕ.[33] Despite this virtue, two problems remain. Here we come to the most demanding part of my argument. The problems that face the present theory are both intricate and difficult—but, in the rest of this section, I show that they can be solved.

The first problem is one of circularity. In giving an account of what it is to act for a reason, we have appealed to the idea of being moved by one's attitude to the reason for which one acts. The attitude in question is desire-like belief. And its content is the fact that one is acting for that reason. But if we have to cite the relation of acting-for-a-reason in our *theory* of acting for a reason, we have moved in a circle—so what has been explained? The second problem is that, as we observed in section 2, one can act for a reason that turns out to be false. Reasons-explanation is non-factive. Consequently, one can believe that A is doing ϕ for the reason that p without being committed to the *truth* of p. This seems to apply even when A is oneself. So on the present account, one can act for the reason that p (and thus believe that one is acting for that reason) without believing that p, and without being in any way committed to its truth. That is surely a mistake. I cannot snap my fingers on the ground that this will make me disappear, if I know perfectly well that it won't happen. My reasons are, in some way or other, constrained by my beliefs. That condition on acting for reasons is not explained by the circular model above.[34]

---

[33] In fact, what is "explained" here is something stronger than *Belief*, and closer to Anscombe's original claim. It leaves out the qualification we derived from Davidson, in section 1. I come back to that issue at the end of section 4.

[34] Note that it *would* be explained by the guise of the good. The claim that something is a good reason to act is factive, so the belief that p is a good reason to ϕ commits one to the truth of p.

The first of these problems, about circularity, is likely to be contentious. There is little agreement about what it takes for an explanatory circle to be vicious. The second problem is more straightforward. As it happens, however, the problems can be solved together, by giving a *psychological* interpretation of acting for reasons. Begin with a simple version, to be refined as we go on:

> To take p as one's reason for doing ϕ is to have the desire-like belief that one is doing ϕ because of the *belief* that p—where this is the "because" of motivation.

On this simple psychological theory, taking something as one's reason is a matter of taking one's belief in that reason to play a causal-motivational role in explaining one's action.[35] (The sense of "motivation" here is the one discussed in section 2.) When I go for a walk outside because the weather is fine, I am motivated by a state that is at once the belief that I am walking outside because I believe that the weather is fine, and like a desire in causing me to do it (and to do it from that belief).[36]

Like the circular model, the simple theory would help to explain *Belief*. But it would also explain the cognitive constraint on *reasons*. In order to act because p, on the simple theory, one must take that consideration as one's reason to act, and in doing so, one must believe that one is motivated by the belief that p. In other words, one must believe that one believes that p.

This claim may be surprising, since our first thought is more mundane: in order to act because p one must believe that p. But, on this point, I think the simple theory is right. To begin with, second-order belief is *necessary* in acting for a reason. No-one can act because p when she is not

---

[35] In making this suggestion, I am deeply indebted to Velleman (1989)—though he argues for it in a rather different way. See also Audi (1986: 82–5) on the capacity of those who act for reasons to explain their action in terms of psychological states that correspond to the reasons for which they act. The central difference between his view and mine is that he does not derive this capacity from a more basic understanding of *taking* something as one's reason, and therefore leaves it insufficiently explained. He is right to say that the self-attribution of reasons has to do with our being *agents*, "not merely well-placed spectators of our own actions" (Audi 1986: 87). But unless we characterize the attitude we take to our reasons as *motivating* or *desire-like*, as well as cognitive, we cannot do justice to this fact. (A second difference is that Audi takes the capacity to explain one's action to be only *typically* present, and so he cannot explain the *necessity* of belief; see Audi 1986: 86.)

[36] To elaborate briefly on the parenthetical clause: it is only when I *take* the fine weather as my reason for walking that my belief about the weather causes me to walk; until I do so, its causal power is muted. So taking something as my reason for doing ϕ is desire-like not only in causing my action, but in causing it to be caused by the relevant belief. If all goes well, it causes its own content to be true. This fact has been exploited in the philosophy of practical reason (principally by Velleman 1989; 2000b) in ways that I examine at the end of Part Two.

aware that she believes that p. Lear may still know that Cordelia loves him more than her sisters, but if he does not realize that he has that belief—he disavows it quite sincerely—its content is not a reason on which he can act. Such hidden beliefs may influence what we do, but not by figuring in what we *take* as our reasons to act.

Is second-order belief *sufficient* for one to act for a reason, even without the first-order belief that p? This is a more delicate issue, but not in a way that threatens the simple psychological theory. It is actually quite difficult to describe a convincing case in which someone believes that they believe that p, without having that belief. When I find it hard to accept that I do not believe that p, wishful thinking and self-deception not only cause me to *believe* that I believe it, they typically cause me to believe it, too. But when this does not happen—when I cannot accept, for instance, that I no longer believe in God, even though I do not—there is a sense in which I can act for a reason I do not believe. I may decide to pray on the ground that God is listening, without in fact believing that he is; it is just that I won't admit to myself that I do not have the relevant belief. In a case like this, as the simple theory claims, I take myself to be moved by a belief I do not have. Since I am wrong about this—I am not moved to act in the way I take myself to be—this counts as at best a marginal case of acting for a reason. We are properly unsure about the description of self-deceptive action. But it does seem possible. It is a strength and not a weakness of the simple theory that it predicts this case, even as it qualifies the principle that one cannot act for a reason one does not believe.

So much for the cognitive constraint on reasons: they must be the objects of second-order belief. In the overwhelmingly typical case, when I act because p, I *rightly* believe that I believe that p, and that this belief is part of what is motivating me to act. This is not to say that it is *all* that is motivating me. We are leaving room for the presence of desire. And we have to leave room, as well, for the motivational role of the desire-like belief involved in taking something as my reason. This points towards a final and somewhat tortuous complication. The simple psychological theory is on the right track, but it gives too weak a content to the attitude of taking-as-one's-reason. It is not sufficient for taking p as my reason for doing ϕ that I take the belief that p to be part of what motivates me in doing it. As we saw in section 2, I can be moved to act by the belief that p without acting for a reason. (Think of the objections to the belief-desire model.) It follows that taking myself to be moved by the belief that p is not sufficient for taking p as my *reason* for doing ϕ, since it does not imply that I take myself to be acting for a reason at all.

It may help to consider an example, adapted from our previous discussion. There we imagined Freud breaking his inkstand, because he believed that his sister would buy him a new one—but not acting *intentionally*.

Now, breaking the inkstand is something he *might* have done intentionally, for that very reason. So let us consider a modified version of the case, in which Freud breaks the inkstand because his sister will then be moved to buy him a new one, and in which he takes the consideration that his sister will buy him a new inkstand as his reason to act. On the simple psychological theory, Freud takes it that he is breaking the inkstand because he believes that his sister will buy him a new one, where this is the "because" of motivation. In other words, he takes himself to be motivated as he was in the original version of the case. But then he need not take himself to be acting for a *reason*, in being moved by this belief; for all he knows, it may be an instance of mere psychological motivation.

In effect, the problem for the simple psychological theory is that it cannot capture the truth in the circular model: to take p as one's reason for doing ϕ is to have the desire-like belief that one is doing ϕ for the *reason* that p, not just that one is doing ϕ because of the belief that p. We already know what is missing here. The belief-desire model went wrong, in section 2, because it gave no account of taking-as-one's-reason, as something essential to the motivation of action done for reasons. If the content of taking-as-my-reason is to depict me as acting for a reason, not just as being motivated by a belief, it must depict me as being motivated by the way I *take* the consideration that p. In other words, the attitude of taking p as my reason to act must present *itself* as part of what motivates my action. The content of taking-as-one's-reason is thus *self-referential*: in acting because p, I take p to be a consideration belief in which motivates me to ϕ *because I so take it*. This attitude *does* depict me as acting for a reason, since it depicts me as being motivated partly by itself, namely by the very fact that I take p as my reason to act.[37] Thus when Freud acts for a reason in breaking the inkstand, in our modified case, he is motivated by a desire-like belief, B, whose content is that he is breaking the inkstand partly because he believes that his sister will buy him a new one, and partly because of B itself. Since this desire-like belief *constitutes* taking the consideration that his sister will buy him a new inkstand as his reason for breaking the old one, it depicts him as being motivated *by* taking that consideration as his reason, and thus as acting for a reason. In what we may think of as the paradigm case of acting for a reason, an agent takes it that he is *hereby* doing ϕ because he believes that p, where this is the "because" of motivation.[38]

[37] In thinking through the issue of self-reference, I have been helped by Harman (1976, section II), Searle (1983: 83–90), and Velleman (1989: 88–90, 94–7, 140–1), who make a similar claim about *intention*. I discuss intention below, in section 4.

[38] A somewhat esoteric complication arises here. We might wish to distinguish between reference to a *token* occurrence of desire-like belief, and reference to the repeatable *state* of having a desire-like belief with such-and-such a content. I am not sure that I understand the idea of a token belief or desire, as opposed to a mental *event*, but in any case, what the

The argument of the last few paragraphs is complicated but its point is basically this: appeal to self-reference permits us to solve the problem of circularity. According to the simple psychological theory:

> To take p as one's reason for doing φ is to have the desire-like belief that one is doing φ because of the *belief* that p—where this is the "because" of motivation.

The refinement about self-reference comes to this:

> To take p as one's reason for doing φ is to have the desire-like belief that one is *hereby* doing φ because of the belief that p.

And if the arguments above are right, this claim captures the truth in the circular model with which we began:

> To take p as one's reason for doing φ is to have the desire-like belief that one is doing φ for the reason that p.

The circular model provides a necessary but not sufficient condition for taking something as one's reason. It is not sufficient because, unlike the psychological theories, above, it cannot explain why our reasons are constrained by our beliefs. It is nevertheless true, on the psychological theory that includes self-reference, that in taking p as one's reason for doing φ, one takes oneself to be acting for that reason, not just to be moved by the relevant belief.[39]

It would be a mistake, I think, to protest that this account makes acting for reasons too reflective or self-conscious. In acting because p one must believe that one believes that p. But this need not be a matter of *conscious* belief.[40] Nor does the claim that we know our reasons for acting, as such, entail that we consciously consider them, or that we must have engaged in deliberation or evaluative reflection, in order to act for reasons. Part of my point has been to *deny* that evaluation is involved in taking some-

---

argument in the main text shows is that taking-as-a-reason must refer to itself, in the explanation of action, as a *state-type*. In order to represent one's action as being done because p, one's desire-like belief must represent it as being done in part because one has a mental state of *this type*—a desire-like belief with this content. Thus when I have the desire-like belief that I am *hereby* doing φ because I believe that p, "hereby" means: by way of being in this mental *state*, or having this mental *property*. It does not matter whether a different *token* of that state or property is what ends up doing the causal work—if, indeed, it makes sense to speak in such terms. This point about the individuation of mental states undermines the argument against self-reference found in Wilson (1989: 278–80).

[39] More carefully, the appeal to self-reference ensures that, in taking p as one's reason for doing φ, one believes something whose truth entails that one is acting for that reason—not that one believes the very proposition that one is doing φ for the reason that p. I think this is close enough.

[40] In saying this, I disagree with those who identify conscious belief with higher-order thought (see, for instance, Mellor 1977–8).

thing as one's reason; the concept of *reason* that figures here is explanatory, not justifying. And in writing about the "reflective" character of acting for reasons, I have had in mind not reflection as an activity of its own, but the fact that a belief about oneself is involved in taking something as one's reason to act. The point is simply that, in acting for a reason, I know what my reason is "spontaneously" or "without observation." While I may not have thought about it consciously, I do not need to investigate myself, as I would another person, in order to give my reason for acting: I already know. Finally, nothing we have said so far implies that practical thought in general—for instance, being swayed by a reason on which one does *not* eventually act—requires the recognition of reasons, as such. There is plenty of room here for responsiveness to reasons (and to considerations that are *not* good reasons) of which we are simply unaware.[41]

Perhaps the most striking claim of the present account is that, in acting for reasons, we have beliefs about the psychological explanation of our action. Curiously enough, this point is anticipated, though misunderstood, by Anscombe. In a neglected discussion, scattered through *Intention* §§8–16, she suggests that some voluntary actions have "mental causes," by which she means that they have "a *cause* known without observation" (1963: 15). In particular, "*intentional* actions are [. . .] subject to mental causality" (1963: 24, my emphasis). Anscombe fails to see the significance of this fact, because she wants to *contrast* mental causes with motives and reasons for acting (1963: 19, 21–2). But her arguments for the contrast are bad. So, for instance, in asking whether an agent's intention in acting is a mental cause, she is led to say "no" because she assumes that mental causes must be *felt* or *experienced* by their agent (1963: 17).[42] It is certainly true that reasons for acting need not correspond to mental causes, in that sense. But they *do* correspond to beliefs we take ourselves to have, and to be moved by, in acting on them.

It is not just a bad philosophy of mind—the illicit focus on what we *feel*—that leads Anscombe to miss the importance of mental causes. She argues elsewhere, on general grounds, that reasons-explanation is not

---

[41] In chapter 2 of *Unprincipled Virtue*, Nomy Arpaly denies that the reasons for which we act must be ones we know, as such (2003: 61). The points made in this paragraph undermine her arguments, which in fact support much weaker claims: first, that *deliberation* is not required in acting for reasons; and second, that we can be moved to act by a belief without *taking* its object as our reason for acting, and thus without acting on the basis of reasons, in the strictest sense (Arpaly 2003: 50–1).

[42] See also Anscombe (1983: 180), where a great deal is made of the fact that thoughts about what one is up to need not "go through one's head," even when they correspond to the reasons one has for doing it.

causal.[43] (I address her arguments in section 5.) And she never stops to ask the questions that her observations raise. *Why* is there such a thing as mental causality? What is it about intentional action that makes knowledge of its causes possible, without observation or inference of any kind? This is the same kind of question as the puzzle about *Belief*, and it finds the beginnings of an answer in the account developed above. There is such a thing as mental causality because, in the paradigm case of acting for a reason, one is moved by a desire-like belief about the explanation of one's action. Mental causality is inextricably tied to our knowledge of the reasons for which we act.

In making this connection with a forgotten aspect of *Intention*, we open up a range of further issues about intentional action. Anscombe's principal example of a mental cause is the feeling of *desire* (1963: 17). By contrast, the arguments of this section have been concerned, almost exclusively, with the role of *beliefs* in what we do for reasons. We have been trying to understand what it is to act because *p*. What about doing something in order to achieve a certain end, or with a further intention, or out of emotion, or for no reason at all? In examining these cases, we will be able to generalize the partial account presented above into a comprehensive theory of intentional action; and we will be able, at last, to provide the full explanation of *Belief*.

4. SOLVING THE PUZZLE

We can begin with another explanation. I have argued that, in the paradigm case of doing φ because *p*, one is moved to act by a self-referential attitude that is at once a belief about why one is doing φ and a desire-like motivation to do it. In going for a walk because the weather is fine, I am moved by the desire-like belief that I am hereby going for a walk because I believe that the weather is fine. I think we can further identify my attitude with the *intention* I have in acting as I do. I intend to be going for a walk, and I intend to be doing so out of the belief that the weather is fine. Our intentions in acting are the desire-like beliefs that figure in making us act. In general, one intends to be doing φ just in case one has the desire-like belief that one is hereby doing it.

Why accept this theory of intention? In part, because it helps to explain the need for intention in acting for reasons. And, in part, because the attitude in question seems to behave like one's intention in acting. There are three points to make about this. First, like intention, it plays a role in *motivating* what one does. Second, it involves the *belief* that one is acting,

---

[43] Anscombe (1983).

and it is often said that intention requires belief.[44] Finally, it is sometimes argued that the content of intention is self-referential: one's intention represents *itself* as part of what motivates action.[45] This is certainly contentious. But once we see that the paradigm case of acting for a reason must involve a desire-like belief that represents itself as causing its agent to act, the theory on which it counts as the *intention* to act is virtually irresistible. Intention is a matter of self-referential desire-like belief.

It is a further argument for this account that it extends in such a natural way to *prospective* intention, or intention for the future. One intends to φ, prospectively, just in case one has the desire-like belief that one is hereby *going* to φ. Prospective intention differs from one's intentions in acting only in that it concerns, not what one is *doing*, but what one is *going* to do. Again we accommodate the motivational role of intention, its alleged connection with belief, and the controversial claim of self-reference.

Having identified intention with desire-like belief, the time has come to address doubts about the very possibility of such a thing, doubts that were set aside at the beginning of section 3. In "The Humean Theory of Motivation," Smith argues that nothing could be, at once, a belief-like representation that p, and a desire-like motivation to act in a way that makes that proposition true. His argument depends on his way of characterizing the difference between (ordinary) belief and desire:

> [A] belief that p is a state that tends to go out of existence in the presence of a perception that *not p*, whereas a desire that p is a state that tends to endure, disposing the subject in that state to bring it about that p. (Smith 1987: 54)

Nothing can combine these conflicting dispositions.

This argument is valid, but is it sound? The problem is that it relies on a dubious claim about the nature of desire. Why must a motivating state be disposed to persist in the presence of a conflicting perception? Suppose I want my house to be cleaned by noon. The perception that it won't be done by then may well extinguish my desire. I will tend to give it up, in favour of one with a practicable object—perhaps to clean the house this afternoon. Nothing rests on this particular example. The point is that we can coherently describe desires that are perceptually constrained. Thus we can imagine someone who tends to want only what it looks to her that she will get, someone whose desires quite often disappear in the face of conflicting perceptions. A motivating state need not be compatible with the perception that its object does not, or will not, obtain.

---

[44] The claim is made by Hampshire and Hart (1958), Harman (1976), and Velleman (1989, ch. 4).

[45] For this claim, see Harman (1976, section II), Searle (1983: 83–90), and Velleman (1989: 88–90, 94–7, 140–1).

We can speculate about the source of Smith's mistake. Since the role of a motivating state is to *change* the world, there is a sense in which it must not be constrained by one's beliefs. The point of desire is to close the *gap* between a picture of the world as it is going to be, and a picture of how one wants it to be. But this observation does not support Smith's claim about the nature of desire. What it supports is something weaker: the desire that *p* must be compatible with the belief that it will not be the case that *p* unless one intervenes. What is problematic is the idea of a motivating state constrained by one's picture of how the world is going to be without one's intervention, a kind of desire whose object can only be something one thinks will come true anyway. Such a state could never be called upon to play its motivational role. It does not follow from this, however, that one's desire that *p* must be compatible with the belief that *not p*, *simpliciter*; or that there is any defect in the theory of intention as motivating or desire-like belief.

These diagnostic thoughts do not explain why Smith appeals to *perception*, instead of just belief, in presenting his theory of desire. The difference may be significant. For to say that one *perceives* that *p* is to suggest that one is presented with the fact that *p* as something that obtains *already*, not just that one expects it to be the case. To perceive that *p* is not merely to predict that *p*, however confidently, but to recognize it as having come to pass. In this light, one might expect the desire that *p* to be *incompatible* with the perception that *not p*, *and* with the perception that *p*. If one comes to see that *p* (or *not p*) is already the case, one will no longer be moved to change it. This suggests a new account of the contrast between belief and desire:[46]

> If S is a desire that *p*, it is disposed to go out of existence in the presence of a perception that *p*—a perception that its work is done.

> If S is a belief that *p*, it is *not* disposed to go out of existence in the presence of a perception that *p*, by which it is merely confirmed.

If these claims are right, then, although his argument is defective, Smith's conclusion may be true, that no state can be belief-like *and* desire-like with respect to the proposition that *p*. But, again, there is a problem in the proposed conception of desire. Think about desires that have the contents I have ascribed to our intentions: the desire to be doing something, or the desire that one is going to do it. Such desires are *not* disposed to disappear in the presence of a perception that their objects are true. If I want to be reading a book, the perception that I am doing so will not lead me to stop. And if there is such a thing as the perception that something is

---

[46] For this proposal, see Piller (1996: 355).

going to happen, it does not interfere with the corresponding desire. It *is* true, of course, that the desire involved in a prospective intention—the desire that one is going to do something—is disposed to vanish when one perceives that one is done. If I want it to be the case that I am going to mow the lawn, and I notice that I have finished, I won't want to do so any more. But this does not mark a contrast between belief and desire. The point applies, in just the same way, to the *belief* that one is going to do something: the belief that I am going to cook dinner tonight is replaced by a belief about the past when I see that the meal has been cooked. There is nothing incoherent in the idea of a desire-like belief whose content is that of an intention to act.

With a theory of intention in hand, we can begin to generalize the account of acting for reasons begun in section 3. There I considered answers to the "why?"-question that consist in giving a fact, or putative fact, as the ground on which someone is acting. To do something because *p* is to be motivated by an explanation of one's action that appeals to belief. It is just as common to explain what one is doing in *teleological* terms. "Why am I turning the key? In order to the start the car."

In the simplest case, one's intention explains what one is doing in terms of a *desire* and the belief that one's action is a means to its satisfaction. Being moved to act by an intention of this kind is, I think, the fundamental form of practical teleology: acting for the sake of an *end*. As I type these words, for the sake of finishing this book, I *take* finishing the book as my reason for typing, and that explains why I am doing it. I am moved to act by the desire-like belief that I am hereby typing out of the desire to finish the book, and the belief that typing is a means to that end. Apart from the content of my intention, this is exactly like the case in which my reason for acting is a putative fact. Indeed, it follows from this picture of acting-with-an-end that, in doing so, one is always acting-for-a-reason, in the previous sense. One's intention appeals to a desire *and* a belief. So, for instance, in typing these words, I am acting on the ground that doing so is a means to finishing the book.

I think of acting-with-an-end as the fundamental form of practical teleology because the more familiar expression, "doing something in order to ϕ," seems to me to have the stronger implication that the agent *intends* and does not merely *desire* to ϕ. In any case, it is at least very often true that when an agent does something in order to ϕ, he acts with the intention of doing ϕ (see Anscombe 1963: 20–3, 34–6). It is a striking fact that we can describe this kind of teleology in several ways.[47] Suppose that John is

[47] Here I am indebted to a forthcoming paper by Michael Thompson, "Naïve Action Theory"—though his account of the teleological explanation of action is radically non-psychological, and is in many ways the opposite of mine.

treating his deck in order to protect it from rain. That is what he intends to do by treating it. It follows from this description that he is treating his deck with the *end* of protecting it from rain, and that his reason for doing so is that he is *going to* protect it from rain. These entailments are explained by the present theory of acting for reasons. John is moved to act by the desire-like belief that he is hereby treating his deck with the *intention* of protecting it from rain. Because the intention to ϕ constitutes a *desire* or *motivation* to ϕ, it follows that he is treating his deck out of the desire to protect it from rain, and therefore with that end. And because the intention to ϕ is a desire-like *belief* that one is going to ϕ, it follows from the account of section 3 that his reason for treating the deck is that he is going to protect it from rain.

Other kinds of explanation are possible. Consider the case in which action is motivated by a minimally informative intention: a desire-like belief that one is hereby doing ϕ that provides no further explanation of one's action. It says nothing about the beliefs and desires by which one is moved to act, except for the reference to itself. Action of this kind is the bare execution of intention—as when I simply decide to stretch my arms, or to kick the leaves at the side of the path as I walk along—and it is not something that is done for a reason. Still, it belongs with what we do for reasons precisely because it shares the structure of motivation by intention. This helps us to explain, and to defend, Anscombe's conviction that one can act intentionally for no particular reason (1963: 25). Intentional action is action of a kind to which the question "why?" has application, understood as a request for reasons (1963: 9). This kind is defined not by the *presence* of reasons, but by the *possibility* of their presence that turns on the role of intention in its motivation. The presence of intention is presupposed when we ask the question "why?" If one has a reason for acting, it will figure in the content of the intention on which one acts. If intention is absent, the question does not apply. And if one acts on an intention that says nothing about the explanation of one's action—besides the reference to itself—one is acting intentionally, but for no particular reason.[48]

In following Anscombe here, we also accommodate what Rosalind Hursthouse calls "arational action": intentional action caused by emotion, and not done for reasons in the ordinary sense—not done *in order to* express the emotion, or to achieve some other effect—but of which it

---

[48] A complication: it follows from the account in this paragraph, together with the previous account of acting on one's intention that, in doing ϕ for no particular reason, one is doing ϕ *in order to* ϕ and the *for the sake of doing* ϕ. I used to regard this as a problem to be solved (as in Setiya 2004c: 391, n. 28), but in fact it is quite correct to say, in such a case, that I am doing ϕ "just for the sake of it" or "just in order to do it."

seems wrong to say that it is done for no reason at all (1991: 57–9). As Hursthouse says, it seems to be done "*qua* expression of emotion" (1991: 61). The present account explains this possibility. When I shout at the Pirates' manager as I listen to the radio, I am acting intentionally—this is not like the case in which I clench my fists without meaning to, or cannot help but smile—but I am not doing so because it makes me feel better, or in order to influence him. Nor am I doing it in order to express my anger; for I need not have that further end (see Hursthouse 1991: 60–1). This is a case in which my intention is a desire-like belief that explains what I am doing in terms of my emotion: I intend to be shouting because I am angry, where this is the "because" of motivation, not of agents' reasons. In other words, I intend to shout out of anger, not simply to do so, for no particular reason. Yet I am not acting for a reason in the sense of acting *because p* or *in order to* ϕ, since my intention does not explain my action in terms of belief or desire. This is why arational action is possible, and how it occupies its curious middle ground between acting for reasons, and doing something for no reason at all.

There is a final complication, which turns on the difficult phenomenon of *trying*. If the story I have been telling so far is right, one would expect that the "why?"-question, understood as a request for reasons, is "refused application by the answer : 'I was not aware that I was doing that'" (Anscombe 1963: 11). In the paradigm case of intentional action, the agent *intends* to act, and this intention involves a belief about what she is doing. The problem, as we saw in section 1, is that there are exceptions to this simple view. That is why I was circumspect in stating the belief requirement:

> *Belief*: When someone is acting intentionally, there must be something he is doing intentionally, not merely trying to do, in the belief that he is doing it.

In Davidson's example, a man is making ten carbon copies intentionally, even though he does not believe that he will succeed; he is merely *trying* to do so (1971: 50; 1978: 91–4). On our account, the carbon-copier does not *intend* to make ten copies, since he does not believe that he is doing so. Still he does it intentionally, and he may do it for reasons. How can we accommodate this case?

The answer is, roughly, that I count as doing ϕ intentionally when I succeed in doing ϕ by doing something else intentionally—taking some means to doing ϕ—precisely with the *end* of doing ϕ.[49] In such a case, I

---

[49] Suppose I know that in doing C, I will be doing E, even though I do not want or intend the latter. Do I count as doing E intentionally? (For discussion of this phenomenon, see Harman 1986, ch. 9; Bratman 1987, ch. 8; and Hanser 1998; 2000.) The present account leaves this question—I think rightly—indeterminate. In cases like this, I think of my reasons for doing C as part of what explains my doing E, and thus attach them to the

am doing φ for the reason that *p* just in case I am taking the means for the reason that *p*, and I have the end of doing φ *because* I believe that *p*, where this is the "because" of motivation. In Davidson's example, the carbon-copier cannot take anything *directly* as his reason for making ten copies, since that would involve the *belief* that he is making ten copies, which he does not have. But if he wants to make ten copies because he believes there are ten people in his class, he can attach that reason to the action of pressing hard on the paper with the *end* of making ten copies, and we can thus regard it as his reason for making ten copies, in a derivative way.

There is a further subtlety in this case, where trying to φ is a matter of doing something for the sake of that end.[50] When an agent tries to φ, in this sense, she counts as doing φ intentionally only if she does it in accordance with her plan. In another example from Davidson, a man tries to kill someone by shooting at him; "the killer misses his victim by a mile, but the shot stampedes a herd of wild pigs that trample the intended victim to death" (1973: 78). Here the gunman kills his victim, but not *intentionally*, even though he kills him by doing something with that end. So an agent's reasons attach to the act that is her end in doing something only if she achieves that end in the right way. The attachment seems to "run through" her conception of *how* she will bring about the end, and it is only this way of bringing it about that constitutes the doing of the end as an intentional act.

This point applies to non-basic action, in general.[51] Suppose I am playing a particular piece of music. This is something I do *by* performing other actions, like playing a passage, or a movement of the piece, and finally by performing *basic* actions, like moving my hand in order to play a note. I need not be performing a basic action at every point while I am playing

---

consequential act, in a certain way. But I "take" them as reasons for doing E only in the epistemic, not the practical sense. (This is true even if I want to do E, so long as I am not doing C with that in mind.) This is why we are unsure what to say about the merely foreseen consequences of intended acts, which lie in the murky zone between what is clearly intentional and what clearly is not. (For a similar claim about such cases, see Hampshire and Hart 1958: 7.)

[50] The idea that trying to do something is typically a matter of doing something else, so that trying not a special *kind* of act, is offered by Jones (1983) as a corrective to Hornsby (1980, ch. 3) and O'Shaughnessy (1973). Note, however, that, as Jones insists, doing something with the end of doing φ is *sufficient* but not *necessary* for trying to φ: when I wake up paralyzed, and decide to move my arm, I *try* to move it, although I do not do anything with that end. It is surprisingly difficult to give a unified account of trying to act that accommodates every case.

[51] Here, and in the remainder of this section, "basic" and "non-basic action" will always refer to basic and non-basic *intentional* action. The qualification is too cumbersome to include in the text.

the piece, since I count as playing it even in the breaks between movements, and the momentary silences as notes hang in the air. It is sufficient
that I am in the *midst* of doing such things. What this comes to in the
typical case is that I *intend* to be playing the piece, and that the further
intentions that motivate the basic actions by which I have been doing so
are motivated, in turn, by that original intention (and by the psychological
states that correspond to my reasons for playing the piece, which it describes).[52] There may be several steps here: I am moving my hands in order
to play a note, which I am doing in order to play a passage, which I am
doing in order to play a movement, and so on. Each step must satisfy the
condition laid out in the previous paragraph: when I am acting with the
end of doing ϕ, I count as doing ϕ intentionally just in case I do it in
accordance with my plan. In this way, a complex motivational structure
of basic actions, like moving one's hands, constitutes the performance of
a non-basic action, like playing a piece of music.

This account of non-basic action may seem too elaborate to characterize much of what we do. Can I really be said to have all these particular
intentions, corresponding to each of the actions by which I play the
music? Note, however, that such intentions are required only if those actions are to be *intentional*, subject to knowledge without observation, and
the application of the question "why?" That need not be so. As habit
takes over, the movements of my fingers become automatic: they are actions I perform, though not intentionally. This may sound odd, but not if
we cancel the implication that they are *un*intentional or involuntary; they
are merely "sub-intentional." As my skills develop, what used to be non-
basic action—playing C sharp by moving my fingers thus-and-so—becomes basic, something that I can simply do. I no longer have any idea
how my fingers are moving, except perhaps through memory, as I play
the notes. Many of the actions we perform have "sub-intentional" components, some of which have never been intentional. There is a distinction
to be drawn among the actions by which I do something intentionally,
between those that are themselves intentional actions, undertaken with
that end, and those that are not. The account in the previous paragraph,
with all its complexity, applies to the first kind of action-as-means, not to
actions of the second, habitual kind.

If this discussion is right, it provides the final explanation of *Belief*. For
while non-basic action may be performed without intention, provided

---

[52] Motivation here is a matter of non-deviant causation, in the sense indicated, at least in
outline, in section 2. I do not mean to add anything to what I said there about the motivation
of *basic* action, and of intention and desire. (The motivation of basic action *by* intention or
desire is a matter of causal *guidance*; and the motivation of intention and desire by other
states of mind depends on the agent's dispositions.) The point of this paragraph is to rely
on those phenomena in order to explain the motivation of *non-basic* action.

that it is the end of something one intentionally does, basic actions must be ones that we intend. If I am not sure that I will succeed in playing a piece of music, I may still do so intentionally, if I play the notes for the sake of that end. But in playing the notes—assuming that this is a matter of basic action—I must intend, and thus be aware of, what I am doing. My intention is what connects my reasons with these actions, and their ends. When I am acting intentionally, there must be something I am doing intentionally, not merely trying to do, in the belief that I am doing it.

5. A Causal Theory of Action?

The purpose of this section is to address some questions that face any account of intentional action that makes use of causal concepts. I hope to say just enough to indicate that the problems can be solved, without working them out in detail.

On the present account, intentional action is motivated, and therefore caused, by one's intention in acting. When one acts for a *reason*, one's intention, in turn, represents one as being moved by belief or desire. If all goes well, one's action is motivated (and therefore caused) by this belief or desire, acting together with one's intention. We have already discussed one problem about the concept of *motivation*: the existence of deviant causal chains. I explained in section 2, albeit in outline, how I think this problem can be solved. But even if I am right, a second problem remains. In "The Causation of Action," Anscombe argues that it is a "mistake [. . .] to think that the relation *being done in execution of a certain intention*, or *being done intentionally*, is a causal relation between act and intention [. . .] intention does not have to be a distinct psychological state which exists either prior to or contemporaneously with the intentional action whose intention it is" (1983: 179–80). Anscombe's discussion makes three points: first, that when one acts intentionally, the thought of what one is doing need not "go through one's head"; second, that one's intention is not always *distinct* from one's action; and third, that it need not *precede* one's action, so as to be its efficient cause. The first point is weak. It depends on the mistake of thinking that intentions must be *conscious* thoughts, the same mistake that we found in Anscombe's discussion of "mental causality" at the end of section 3. But the other points are more significant; they serve to complicate the treatment of intention as a cause of intentional action.

As the second point insists, we cannot always separate one's intention from one's intentional action. In some cases, the intention is a necessary condition of the action, so that there is no way to decompose that action into parts, with intention as the cause of a "*pre*-intentional act," of a kind that may or may not be intentional.[53] So, for instance, dropping one's keys is something one can do intentionally or not; but such things as greeting and promising are only possible as the execution of intentions (see Anscombe 1963: 84–5). In cases like these, the intention is not fully distinct from the action, which is impossible without it. It does not follow, however, that it cannot be its cause. That inference turns on an excessively narrow conception of efficient causation. When one is doing φ because one intends to be doing it, it may be true that one could not be doing it without that intention, yet still be true that one's intention plays an efficient-causal role in its own execution. If I cannot make a promise without intending to do so, still I can make the promise because I so intend.

Anscombe's final point is that one's intention in acting need not exist *before* one begins to act, and therefore cannot be the efficient cause of intentional action since causes precede their effects. Here I think she is partly right. As I have argued, intention involves belief, so that when I intend to be running, I believe that I am doing so. It follows that this intention cannot precede the action it depicts, on pain of being *false*, at least to begin with. And it follows, in turn, that one's intention in acting cannot be the efficient cause of one's *beginning* to act. This is not a problem for my account. It is perfectly true that I do not *begin* to raise my arm because I intend to *be* raising it, or do so "in execution" of that intention. Beginning to do something is one thing, doing it another. What matters for my account is that, once I have started doing something, we can say that I am doing it intentionally because I intend to be doing it: intention plays a causal role in sustaining intentional action, as it goes on.

These remarks help to clarify, and to qualify, the sense in which I am defending a causal theory of intentional action. I have been trying to explain what is involved in *doing* something intentionally, without worrying about how one began. In acting intentionally, one is moved to act by an intention that explains what one is doing. Being moved to act is, *inter alia*, being *caused* to act. To that extent, this counts as a causal theory of action. It differs from other causal theories, however, in that it is concerned with the causal process that accompanies action, not with what precedes it.[54] The causal constraint on acting intentionally does not concern the *origin* of one's action, but its being caused by one's intention (and in accordance with the content of that intention) as it goes on.[55]

---

[53] As I understand it, this is the proper moral to draw from the obscure and confusing argument of Anscombe (1963: 28–9).

[54] Here I follow Frankfurt (1978).

[55] The phenomenon I am describing here is not confined to intentional action. So, for instance, we say that the chocolate is melting because it is heating up, or that the crops are dying because there is a drought. Even if it is true in these cases that the heating precedes the chocolate's beginning to melt and the drought began before the crops started to die, we do not insist on this temporal order in describing the causal relation between them, as it

Matters are different when we consider the *beginning* of action. As I stressed above, whether one began doing something intentionally is a separate question from whether one is doing it intentionally now. I may begin to act intentionally, but end up "in automatic." (How did I get home? What route did I take? I have no idea. I just found myself here.) Likewise, I may begin doing something unintentionally, but then decide to go on. (I am not sure when I started tapping my feet to the music, but now I'm doing it for fun.) In much the same way, the *reasons* for which one began to do something are sometimes different from the reasons for which one is doing it now. We can apply the arguments of section 3 and section 4 to the case of beginning to act.[56] Setting aside complications about trying, one *begins* doing ϕ *intentionally* just in case one is moved to begin doing ϕ by the desire-like belief that one is hereby going to begin. If one's beginning to act is itself intentional, one's intention to begin is the cause of one's intentional action. Similarly, in order to have *reasons* for beginning to do something, one must *intend* to begin doing it for those reasons, and thereby *take them* as one's reasons for beginning. In this case, unlike the ones discussed in the previous paragraphs, one's intention *does* precede its own execution, and it is, in the ordinary way, its efficient cause.

This point about temporal precedence applies to prospective intention, in general. When I intend to do something in the future, I have the desire-like belief that I am going to do it, and when I act on this intention, it is a cause of my intentional action. Claims like this are apt to generate a dubious picture, of forming an intention as lighting the fuse of a bomb that will simply detonate when the time is right. But a causal theory of prospective intention need not carry that implication; it does not follow that we are *passive* when we act on our intentions. In fact, the theory of section 4 suggests exactly the opposite. In order to act now on the basis of a prospective intention, one must *take* one's intention as one's reason for acting. One's attitude to that intention is active and, in a modest sense, reflective: one must be aware of one's intention in order to act on it. That seems to me exactly right: if I forget that I intend to file my taxes tomorrow, I won't end up doing it. We have to keep track of our prospective intentions, and whether we act on them or not is up to us.[57]

---

now obtains. What we state is a causal relation between two concurrent goings-on, like the causal relation between one's intention in acting and one's action. The proper theory of this relation ought to make sense of the claims I am making in the text.

[56] The account in this paragraph applies, more generally, to actions that lack (perceptible) duration, as when I cough because I intend to do so right now. Here, it may be argued, there is no period during which one intends to be *doing* ϕ: one simply intends to ϕ, prospectively, and one is motivated to do it.

[57] To say that this is "up to us" is of course consistent with giving our intentions a defeasible role in causing us to act.

There is more to be said about the causal structure of intentional action. For instance, it is significant that, while reasons correspond to psychological causes, these causes are made effective by one's intention in acting, or one's intention to begin. The desire-like belief, that I am hereby doing φ because I believe that p, is desire-like or motivating not only with respect to my doing φ, but in causing it to be the case that I am doing it because of that belief. It is because I intend to act on my belief that p that this belief is causing me to act. In the typical case, it would not do so if I had no such intention. (Note that this counterfactual test for causation is only approximate; one's intention may be an *over-determining* cause.) In effect, the whole causal process of acting for a reason, including the causal role of the belief whose content is my reason or the desire whose content is my end, depends on what I intend to do. Our reasons for acting are up to us, in that their causal role depends on our intention—whatever the cause of that intention itself.

This result will be welcomed by the *incompatibilist*, who doubts that freedom can be reconciled with causal determination, but who wants to make sense of acting for reasons nonetheless. It is sometimes argued that this cannot be done: an agent acts for reasons only so far as they correspond to causes that determine his action.[58] But if the arguments above are right, this is beside the point. It may be true that reasons correspond to determining causes, but they are causes that operate only when one intends them to—and one's intention need not be determined or even caused. This is not to say that the present account *depends* on indeterminism, or that it conflicts with a compatibilist conception of freedom in action. But the fact that it might be *used* by the incompatibilist points to what is distinctive about its causal character. It is, in the first place, a theory about the causal process that *constitutes* intentional action, or acting for a reason, not about the causes that come before.

6. AGAINST THE GUISE OF THE GOOD

In section 3, I began to make a case against the claim that reasons for action must be seen under the guise of the good. In effect, my argument had two sides. On the one hand, I claimed that this doctrine is redundant: it does not help us to explain *Belief*; and the sufficient conditions of acting

---

[58] This kind of argument is often traced to Hume's *Treatise* (2.3.2), and, more recently, to Hobart (1934). The reply suggested in the main text partly resembles one proposed by Carl Ginet (1989). He argues that reasons are attached to our actions by our *intentions*, not by cause-and-effect. I agree with the first part of his claim, but not the second, which ignores the causal role of intention itself.

for a reason, which *do* explain *Belief*, do not require it. On the other hand, I tried to diagnose its false appeal. It will be tempting to us if we recognize the defects of the standard belief-desire model of intentional action, but see the guise of the good as the only alternative there is. That is an easy mistake to make—for instance, if one sees that acting for a reason involves *taking* something as one's reason to act, and one assumes that "reason" figures here in its normative or justifying sense. As I have argued, however, that interpretation is false. Taking something as one's reason cannot simply be a matter of taking it as a *good* reason to act. That would make a mystery of *Belief*. Instead, it is a matter of taking something as a reason that *explains* one's action. We can make sense of this, without circularity, and without the guise of the good, in causal-psychological terms. In doing so, we solve the problems that sank the standard model, we find a place for intention in intentional action, and we provide the deep explanation of *Belief*.

 It follows from these arguments that acting for a reason is not a matter of acting under the guise of the good. It is not just that there seem to be cases in which one thinks one's reason is bad or worthless, as at the end of section 2, but that, in general, we can say what is involved in acting for a reason without appeal to normative or evaluative thoughts. I can act because I *take* something as my reason for acting, and thus act *for that reason*, without taking the reason to be good.

In framing this view, I have relied on a conceptual distinction between the sense of "reason" that figures in claims about what there is *good* reason to do, and the sense that figures in claims about the reasons for which we actually do things. Although this distinction is familiar, it is still quite commonly ignored. Thus in defending his version of the guise of the good, Joseph Raz protests against the attempt to "[explain] reasons independently of value," asking whether it can "preserve the normativity of reasons": "Does it account for the fact that defying reasons is irrational, that one may disregard a reason only to follow a more stringent one?" (1999: 28). The claim that defying reasons is irrational must be heard as a claim about normative or justifying reasons.[59] If we are talking about the reasons for which we act, it barely makes sense to speak of someone "defying a reason." Something counts as my reason for acting only if I *act* on it, and therefore do not "defy it." At the very least, it is question-begging to assume, as Raz does, that explanatory reasons must be understood in normative terms.

A more subtle mistake is made by Korsgaard, in "The Normativity of Instrumental Reason." She is right to reject the standard model: "neither

---

[59] Even then, it is misleading, as I have argued elsewhere (Setiya 2004a).

the joint causal efficacy of [belief and desire], nor the existence of an appropriate conceptual connection between them, nor the bare conjunction of these two facts" is sufficient for intentional action. And she goes on to say—again, quite plausibly—that in acting intentionally, an agent "must be motivated by her own *recognition* of the appropriate conceptual connection between the belief and the desire." Something like this is true, not of intentional action in general, but of what we do for reasons: we are moved to act by higher-order thoughts—intentions, or desire-like beliefs—about our own beliefs and desires. But it does not follow, as Korsgaard suggests, that intentional action is "motivated by [. . .] the *rational necessity* of doing something."[60] To say that we decide upon our reasons is not to say that we decide that they are *good* or *decisive* reasons, just that we decide that they will be the reasons on which we act. Intentional action is "reflective" because it involves desire-like beliefs about itself: it is *reflexive*, not essentially evaluative.[61]

I began this part of the book by tracing the guise of the good to Platonic and Aristotelian claims about desire. But our focus narrowed quickly. For the most part, I have been arguing against a claim about our reasons for acting, according to which we must regard them as doing something to *justify* our action. We have seen that there is no need for this, and that it turns on confusions and mistakes about the concept of a reason. It remains to ask whether there is anything to be salvaged from the intuitions that lie behind this version of the guise of the good. Is there some other, more modest, but still significant, sense in which intentional action aims at the good?

Our first thought may be to go back to Plato and Aristotle. In acting intentionally, one acts on the basis of *desire*, and desire presents its object in a favourable light. Thus a kind of positive evaluation, however minimal, is always directed at what one intentionally does. Influential though it may be, I think this argument is really quite weak. There may be species of "desire"—what Johnston (2001) calls "affects"—that are tied to specific evaluative categories, things like finding someone attractive, being captivated by a book, or being bored with one's work. But there is no reason

---

[60] The quotations in this passage are from Korsgaard (1997: 221). (I find a similar slide in her earlier book; see Korsgaard 1996: 93–4, 113.) Note that the official topic of Korsgaard (1997) is "rational action," but I take it that she means by this not "perfectly rational action," but "action of the kind characteristic of rational agents"—namely, *intentional* action.

[61] This claim gives qualified support to Frankfurt's (1988) conception of autonomy as a matter of higher-order volition or desire. The qualification is that my topic is intentional action, as such, not "autonomous action" or action with which one "identifies." I am not sure that I understand these more demanding notions.

to think that desire in that sense is always involved in intentional action. What is true is that, if one is doing something intentionally, one is moved by one's intention in acting, and since intention is a matter of desire-like belief, one is, in the corresponding sense, moved by desire. The sense of "desire" in question here simply registers the fact that intentions are able to motivate action. They need not involve any particular experience of value. I may decide to act on a groundless impulse, or for no reason at all.

It is worth being careful, here, about *trivialized* versions of the guise of the good, on which the point is simply to find a role for desire, in whatever minimal sense, in every case of intentional action. I agree that there is such a role, for the reason I gave a moment ago. But it is very misleading to report this fact in evaluative terms. I think Davidson is guilty of this. So, for instance, he says that intentional action is always caused by a "pro-attitude" which represents what the agent finds desirable about his action (Davidson 1963: 9). But when he argues, in later work, that this pro-attitude is required, his point is simply that, when someone is moved to act by a belief, he must be *disposed* to act on the basis of that belief, where "[this] disposition is what I mean by a pro-attitude" (Davidson 1987: 108). In order to secure the need for a pro-attitude in the explanation of action, Davidson is forced to drain it of evaluative content; it is a mere disposition. On this interpretation, there is no *substance* to the claim that intentional action aims at the good. (I return to the topic of desire in Part Two, section 4.)

A final suggestion is possible: that the truth behind the guise of the good is that reasons-explanation makes action *intelligible*, that this is missing from the account developed above, and that it can only be captured in normative or evaluative terms. This line of thought has several threads, which I will try to pull apart.

One claim is that the appeal to intelligibility supports the guise of the good in something like the form with which we began. This way of approaching the matter is suggested by Raz:

> [Typical] intentional actions are actions about which their agents have a story to tell [. . .] It is a story which shows what about the situation or action made it, the action, an intelligible object of choice for the agent, given who he is and how he saw things at the time. [. . . The] task of explaining human agency is precisely the task of making sense of this common assumption. The classical approach [which accepts the guise of the good] is one route one can follow in attempting such an explanation. According to it the 'story' is of what the agents took to be facts which show the act to be good, and which therefore constitute a reason for its performance. (Raz 1999: 24)

Raz goes on to argue that *only* the "classical approach" can account for the fact that explanation by reasons makes action intelligible. I doubt, however, that the pre-theoretic notion of "intelligibility" can carry so much weight; and so I doubt that its articulation serves as a constraint on the theory of acting for reasons, just as such. In the ordinary sense of the word, acting for a reason—even a reason one sees as good—is not always intelligible; and intentional action can be made intelligible without appeal to reasons, in that sense.

For the first point, imagine someone who is relentlessly and indiscriminately rude. He seems to have no sense whatsoever of the effect of his brusque approach on others, and when he is aware of it, he could not care less. If he one day decides to tone down his complaints in order spare my feelings, because he believes that he should do so, I am liable to find his action unintelligible, even though it is done for a reason he sees, suddenly and inexplicably, under the guise of the good. His behaviour makes no sense. Has there been some conversion experience? Perhaps someone was rude to him, in return, and he realized how it feels. But no: it is a one-off case, and nothing has happened to change him. Acting out of character in this way can be unintelligible, even when it meets the conditions of the "classical approach."

For the second point—intelligibility without good reasons—we can turn to "arational action" (Hursthouse 1991). In the ordinary sense of the word, it is perfectly *intelligible* when people hit inanimate objects in anger, jump up and down in excitement, or tear their clothes in grief, even if they are not acting for reasons at all. This is intelligible not just in being something we might predict, but because we can understand it "from the inside." The same is true of acting from *spite*, for instance, and of my decision to smoke a whole pack of cigarettes tonight, since I am quitting at midnight—even though I see nothing to be said for doing so. It is often quite easy to understand why people act in ways they do not see as good. In both directions, then, the connection between evaluation and intelligibility, in the ordinary sense, is loose.

When philosophers appeal to that connection, however, they may have something more technical in mind. According to John McDowell:

> [The] concepts of the propositional attitudes have their proper home in explanations of a special sort: explanations in which things are made intelligible by being revealed to be, or to approximate to being, as they rationally ought to be. This is to be contrasted with a style of explanation in which one makes things intelligible by representing their coming into being as a particular instance of how things generally tend to happen. (McDowell 1985: 328)

Here the concept of intelligibility is given a distinctive spin: the claim is that "[a] reason is a rational cause" (Davidson 1974: 233), and that explanation by reasons is "rationalizing" in that it shows the agent as having engaged in something approaching good practical thought. In this qualified sense, the argument goes, intentional action does take place under the guise of the good.

It is essential to speak of "approximation" here. It would not be plausible to claim, as Dancy does, that when we "explain an action [. . .] we show that it would have been [what there was most reason to do] if the agent's beliefs had been true" (2000: 9). That would imply that, except when we are mistaken about our circumstance, we always do what there is most reason to do. In other words: whatever our circumstance, we never engage in bad practical thought.[62] If there is a connection between the explanation and justification of action, it cannot be anywhere near as close as that. Dancy eventually backs away from his initial claim, saying instead that "the aim of [seeing the agent's reasons as good ones] stands as what one might call a regulative ideal for the explanation of action" (2000: 95).

That is certainly more plausible than saying, in effect, that our actions are always justified, in light of our beliefs. But it is still a puzzling claim. Why accept that the motivation of imperfectly rational beings, like us, must be explained in each case by its resemblance to good practical thought, as though our failures are mere perturbations of a system that is otherwise ideal? If it is possible to act for a reason that is no good at all—not a good reason to act in any situation whatsoever—it is hard to see what sense to give to the claim that, in doing so, one tends towards good practical thought. Like the simple view addressed in the previous paragraph, McDowell's claim about the explanation of action seems to place unrealistic constraints on how bad our practical thought can be.

I do not mean that there are no constraints on this at all. The idea that reasons-explanation is "rationalizing" in a normative sense derives its plausibility from the fact that we cannot go wrong without limit. The question is how this limit applies. Some authors make claims of strict impossibility for thoroughly defective forms of practical thought. Thus, according to Raz, it is obvious that "I cannot choose to have coffee because I love Sophocles" (1997: 8). And, in a well-known discussion, Thomas Nagel contrasts the intelligibility of being moved to put a dime in a slot by the desire for a drink and the belief that this is a vending machine with the case in which that belief and desire cause me to put a dime in my pencil sharpener (see Nagel 1970: 33–4). According to Nagel, the latter case must involve "deviant causation," not genuine motivation, because it is so far from corresponding to good practical thought. The fact that I could get the drink I want from a nearby vending machine cannot be my *reason* for putting a dime in my pencil sharpener.

On my account, such cases are not strictly impossible. The (non-deviant) motivation of desire is a matter of one's *dispositions*, and one can

[62] At least not in our dispositions to act on the basis of our beliefs. For this connection, see the first section of the introduction, above.

act for any reason that corresponds to a belief by which one is disposed to be moved.[63] This may seem to be a serious objection. "A theory of motivation is defective if it renders intelligible behaviour which is not intelligible" (Nagel 1970: 34). But, in fact, I think my theory gets it right. Our initial reaction to Nagel's case, and to drinking coffee because one loves Sophocles, is that they are not possible—as, indeed, they are not, in the absence of dispositions that almost nobody has. We assume that these dispositions are missing, and thus that the causal stories are deviant. Once the dispositions are supplied, however, the possibilities in question seem bizarre, but real. Imagine, for instance, that I have been conditioned to put a dime in my pencil sharpener when I believe that I could get the drink I want from a nearby vending machine. This has become a stable tendency of mine. Strange though it is, I can now be *motivated* to put a dime in my pencil sharpener by the relevant belief. And it is not impossible for me put a dime in my pencil sharpener on the ground that I could get the drink I want from a nearby vending machine. (An odd decision, but there it is.) What is true is that—for reasons I am about to explain—such cases are necessarily rare, and that, when they occur, I will typically reject my own behaviour as irrational and consequently give it up. As a *local* phenomenon, however, it is possible to be moved in ways that do not even tend towards good practical thought.

The crucial distinction here is between the existence of normative limits on thought and desire, which I accept, and the (alleged) normativity of reasons-explanation, which I do not. The first phenomenon is tied to Davidson's influential remarks about the "constitutive ideal of rationality" (1970b: 223). In order to have psychological states at all, one must display some level of competence in one's theoretical and practical thought.

> The semantic contents of attitudes and beliefs determine their relations to one another and to the world in ways that meet at least rough standards of consistency and correctness. Unless such standards are met to an adequate degree, nothing can count as being a belief, a pro-attitude, or an intention. (Davidson 1987: 114)

This claim is quite consistent with the theory of action defended here. One's profile of beliefs, desires and dispositions is subject to the constitutive ideal of rationality: one's ways of thought cannot be *too* messed up.[64]

---

[63] For the first point, see the discussion of causation in the belief-desire model, in section 2; for the second point, see the argument for a psychological interpretation of taking-as-one's-reason, in section 3.

[64] Nothing I say here depends on the *strength* of the constitutive ideal—on the *extent* to which one's beliefs, desires and dispositions must be rational. All I need is the fact that there are limits. For a deflationary view of where these limits are, see Cherniak (1986).

That is why, although I can choose to drink coffee because I love Sophocles, so long as I have the appropriate disposition, I cannot always operate
in such defective ways. Taken in general, my dispositions of practical
thought must be quite good if I am to count as a rational being at all.
(That is why I said, in the previous paragraph, that thoroughly defective
cases must be rare.) It does not follow that reasons-explanation itself appeals to the standards of good practical thought, or that it cannot proceed
in merely dispositional terms. It is just that, by and large, the dispositions
must be sensible ones to have.

The mistake is to go from a general claim to one about particular cases.
In general, the dispositions that govern intentional action must approximate the standards of good practical thought. There is pressure for one's
dispositions, taken together, to be at least moderately good. But there
is no reason to suppose that, in each instance, practical thought or the
motivation of action must be "made intelligible by being revealed to be,
or to approximate to being, as [it] rationally ought to be" (McDowell
1985: 328), or that a special kind of explanation is involved. In a given
case, one's reason for acting may be simply and irredeemably bad, with no
resemblance to anything that could count as good or adequate in practical
thought. And it may be explained by the corresponding disposition, not
in essentially normative terms. The constitutive ideal of rationality operates on the whole, not in connection with each episode of practical
thought. Within the limits set by this ideal, it *is* possible to act for reasons
that strike the rest of us as irrelevant or mad. People do act in ways we
find unintelligible, and they can act for *reasons* that we find unintelligible,
too. Explanation by reasons makes action intelligible only in the trivial
sense of *explaining* it; the explanation need not be edifying, or justifying,
and it need not take place, in any sense, "under the guise of the good."[65]

If what I have argued is right, we can do justice to the reflexive or
reflective character of acting for reasons, and to the fact that it is subject
to normative limitations, without conceding that reasons-explanation is

---

[65] It is not clear to me what Davidson himself believes about the normativity of reasons-
explanation. Despite saying that "[a] reason is a rational cause" (Davidson 1974: 233), he
never draws a general contrast between the explanation of action, and the "style of explanation in which one makes things intelligible by representing their coming into being as a
particular instance of how things generally tend to happen" (McDowell 1985: 328). What
he denies is the possibility of *strict* psychological laws, in an exceptionally demanding sense,
not appeal to dispositions and tendencies, and their corresponding "laws" (see Davidson
1987: 111–2). What is more, in arguing that reasons-explanations "differ from physical
explanations," his point is that "in explaining action, we are identifying the phenomena to
be explained, and the phenomena that do the explaining, as directly answering to [. . .]
norms" (Davidson 1987: 114–5). This can be read as a claim about the constitution of
psychological states, including our dispositions, not about the character of the *relations*
among them invoked in the explanation of action.

normative itself. One can act for a reason one does not see as good. Taking something as one's reason is taking it to be a reason that explains what one is doing, not a reason that justifies it. And one's motivation in acting need not be understood through its resemblance to what is good in practical thought.

In Part Two of this book, I examine the ethical implications of pulling these issues apart. As I will argue, the nature of intentional action has little or nothing to say about the *standards* of practical thought. In that sense, the theory of action is an ethical failure: it cannot provide a foundation for practical reason; ethical rationalism is false. The twist is that practical reason itself is not undermined. It does not collapse for lack of an action-theoretic ground. Instead, it is pulled up by the gravity of ethical virtue: the standards of practical reason are standards of good character, applied to practical thought.

PART TWO

Why Virtue Matters to the Study of Practical Reason

IT IS A COMMONPLACE that you get to know people's characters only partly and imperfectly in seeing how they act. Through ignorance and inadvertence, their actions may not correspond to their intentions. And even when they do, what they tell us is limited. How did they reach this decision? How do they feel about it? Would they do the same thing again?

The first of these three questions concerns the connection between an agent's character and the content of her practical thought. This can have a complex texture, as in the following narrative:

> Marge is taking the Tube home on a crowded day. There are no seats left—Marge is sitting in one of them—and several people are standing. In front of Marge, there is a woman with a child in a pram and several shopping bags, struggling but just about coping with her various burdens. Marge notices the woman, but for a while she does not really take in her discomfort; it takes her quite some time to see that the woman could do to take the weight off her feet. Marge decides not to stand. What is she thinking? First, that she'll be getting off in a few stops anyway, so the woman will only have to stand until then. Second, that she's quite tired herself. And third, that there are plenty of younger people sitting down; Marge thinks that one of *them* ought to get up and offer a seat. It is really their job to do it, and quite unfair for Marge—who really is a little tired, as I said—to have to take up the "moral slack."

In this stretch of practical reasoning, Marge is at first insensitive—when she fails to take in the woman's discomfort—then self-serving. It does her no credit that she thinks, "I'll get off in a few stops, so she only has to stand five more minutes," rather than "I'll get off in a few stops, so I might as well stand the last five minutes." She is unscrupulous, too, cooking up a moral justification for laziness, and disguising her selfishness as righteous indignation with the other passengers. It is not just that Marge ought to have offered a seat, and did not do so. Her practical thought goes wrong in distinctive ways.

This is not an isolated case. We constantly make evaluations of character on the basis of practical thought, and apply to it such terms as "selfish," "generous," "callous," and "just." We criticize the character of people whose treatment of moral questions is impoverished or excessively simple, who cannot see a project to completion, or who find it hard to pay attention to anyone else. There is a risk that we will be shamed, not just by our bad decisions, but by the thinking that led to them. That is why we sometimes lie to ourselves and others about our motives, and about the arguments that really move us to behave as we do.

I said in the introduction that one could think of this book as an attempt to determine how practical reason should be understood, when we reject the guise of the good. From a different angle, it might be seen as working out the consequences of the fact that dispositions of practical thought are traits of character, and so can be a matter of ethical virtue and vice. This fact, which I discuss below in section 1, is the basis of a systematic argument for the virtue theory of practical reason.

The Virtue Theory: Being good as a disposition of practical thought is being a disposition of practical thought that is good as a trait of character.

The key to the argument is a claim, in section 2, about the metaphysics of *being good*. The question is whether we can distinguish the property of being good as a disposition of practical thought from the property of being good as a trait of character, applied to those dispositions. I argue that, for this distinction to make sense, the standards of practical reason must derive, at least in outline, from the nature of agency or practical thought. The claim that this derivation is possible—though it need not be comprehensive—is what I call "ethical rationalism."[1] So the task of section 2 is to show that ethical rationalism is the *only* alternative to the virtue theory of practical reason. In doing so, it helps to clarify the *content* of ethical rationalism, and to define the project of the rest of the book.

That project is to argue that ethical rationalism is false, so that the virtue theory is true. I begin by examining the most prominent forms of rationalism: the view that practical thought has a special subject-matter, from which its standards derive; the idea that it deploys normative concepts that place it under distinctive formal constraints; the form of "internalism" on which good practical thought is explained in terms of capacities that "[belong] to the subjective motivational set of every rational being" (Korsgaard 1986: 328); the picture of practical thought as driven by desire; and, finally, the claim that its standards derive from the possibility of "practical knowledge"—the fact that, in acting for reasons, we know what we are doing and why. The first strategy is a "recognitional" conception of practical reason, sometimes associated with Aristotle.[2] The second and third are broadly Kantian.[3] The fourth is instrumentalist.[4] And

[1] See the introduction, section 2.
[2] See, for instance, Cullity and Gaut (1997: 4–5).
[3] Kant (1785; 1788); Nagel (1970); Korsgaard (1986; 1996).
[4] Williams (1980); Dreier (1997).

the fifth and last is pursued by David Velleman, in *Practical Reflection* and *The Possibility of Practical Reason*.[5] In each case, the standards of practical reason are meant to derive, at least in outline, from the nature of agency or practical thought.

In section 3, I argue against both Kantian and Aristotelian forms of rationalism about practical reason. They depend upon claims about agency discredited by the arguments of Part One. More generally, those arguments restrict the materials to which the rationalist can appeal: the capacity to act for reasons depends on little more than *intention* and *motivation*. These elements correspond to the forms of rationalism that occupy the rest of my discussion. In section 4, I argue that the instrumentalist conception of practical reason as means-end efficiency cannot derive from the role of desire in motivation and practical thought. And in section 5, I argue that the foundation for practical reason cannot lie in the involvement of self-knowledge with the intention to act.

On the surface, the strategy here is one of argument by elimination. That is partly right: I think we can undermine the appeal of ethical rationalism by showing that it fails in its most familiar and plausible forms. But an argument *purely* by elimination threatens to be incomplete. So I also try to show, in general, that the arguments of Part One leave no room for the rationalist project to succeed. I argue for this at several points— in particular, at the end of section 5. (I anticipate those remarks at the end of sections 3 and 4.) If I am right, my critical arguments are enough to support a categorical claim, that the standards of practical reason cannot derive, not even in outline, from the nature of agency or practical thought. The ethical rationalist has a bad conception of what it is to be good as a disposition of practical thought. And since ethical rationalism is the only alternative to the virtue theory of practical reason, as I argue in section 2, it follows in turn that the virtue theory is true.

Before I defend this conclusion, I need to do two things. The first is to elaborate, and explain, a preliminary claim: that dispositions of practical thought are traits of character. The second is to examine, in more detail, the *application* of the virtue theory—to give some texture to the abstract formulation above. Both tasks can be pursued through the moral psychology of virtue.

1. CHARACTER AND PRACTICAL THOUGHT

My starting point is a claim established in Part One: that we can act for reasons we do not see as good. More generally, in taking something as

[5] Velleman (1989; 2000b).

one's reason, one takes it to be a reason in the explanatory, not the normative or justifying sense.

What goes for the reasons we act on, and therefore *take* as reasons,
surely goes for the rest of practical thought. If acting for a reason does
not require one to deploy the concept of justification—despite its reflexive
character—the same is true of deliberation as an intentional activity, of
being moved by reasons without consciously considering them, and of the
forming and revising of intentions and desires. The guise of the good is
most plausible when it is applied to the reasons we actually adopt. If it
does not apply to them, it does not apply elsewhere. This is not to deny,
of course, that there is such a thing as asking oneself explicitly what one
should do, and, at least when it is directed at action, and is not merely
hypothetical, this counts as practical thought. The point is that we can
be moved by reasons, form intentions and act on them, solve practical
problems, and change our plans, without asking whether we are justified
in doing so. Practical thought is not always *explicit*: it does not always
deploy the concept of a reason to act.

This fact helps us to be clear about the motivation of the virtuous person. In *Natural Goodness*, Philippa Foot presents an appealing picture of
the virtues of character on which they consist, primarily, in dispositions
of practical thought.

> What, for instance, distinguishes a just person from one who is unjust? The fact
> that he keeps his contracts? That cannot be right, because circumstances may
> make it impossible for him to do so. Nor is it that he saves life rather than
> kills innocent people, for by blameless mishap he may kill rather than save. 'Of
> course,' someone will say at this point, 'it is the just person's intention, not
> what he actually brings about, that counts.' But why not say, then, that it is the
> distinguishing characteristic of the just that *for them certain considerations
> count as reasons for action, and as reasons of a given weight?* Will it not be the
> same with other virtues, as for instance for the virtues of charity, courage, and
> temperance? (Foot 2001: 12)

We can see now that this is ambiguous. To say that "certain considerations count as reasons" for the just person may be to ascribe an explicit
belief that these considerations are good reasons to act, and reasons of
a certain weight, with a consequent disposition to be moved by them.
Or it may simply involve the latter disposition, a tendency to give weight
to certain considerations, in deciding what to do—perhaps without evaluating them at all. Both alternatives describe ways in which possession
of an ethical virtue might turn essentially on dispositions to engage in
certain sorts of practical thought: to treat certain things as reasons, explicitly or not.

Take, for instance, the virtue of benevolence, the core of which is a (no doubt qualified) disposition to be moved by others' needs. Even if we cannot assume that the benevolent agent has a positive belief about the justification of his actions, he surely cannot believe that others' needs *do not* provide him with reasons to act. Someone who thinks that other people are not worth bothering about and do not merit his concern is not properly benevolent, even if he spends his time helping them, and cares about them in what is otherwise just the right way. Benevolence is to be characterized partly in terms of our explicit practical thought. (Again, practical thought counts as explicit, in my sense, just when it deploys the concept of a reason to act.)

Most commonly, I think, our virtuous dispositions make no explicit appeal to justification or practical reason. Consider Beth, who is working out the batting order of the inter-mural softball team, and who is moved only by her beliefs about people's hitting style and ability, and how often they went to bat last week; she is indifferent to her personal attachments and rivalries. In acting as she does, Beth need not think about justice, or about reasons, as such, but she exhibits the virtue of justice, at least to some degree.

Dispositions of this kind—ones concerned with practical thought that is not explicit—are not relevant only to partial or imperfect possession of an ethical virtue. The fully just or benevolent agent is not merely one who has, and is infallibly guided by, a certain set of beliefs about reasons. To think otherwise is to confuse virtue with one kind of *continence*. I think this comes out in Bernard Williams' complaint that the husband who dives in to save his drowning wife because he thinks he *should* goes in for "one thought too many" (1976: 18). If my friend is left cold by the prospect of helping me when I need help, and only does so when he concludes that there is good reason to help—since we are friends—I will begin to doubt his sincerity. Although his actions accord with the virtue of friendship, his thoughts do not. The problem is that he is moved by my needs only *conditionally*, only because he thinks he ought to be. I think it is a general fact about the virtues of character that they go beyond this kind of conditional motivation. Even when the full possession of a virtue involves beliefs about what there is reason to do, it also involves the disposition to be moved *directly* and *unconditionally* by beliefs whose objects are the reasons themselves.[6] A virtuous person's motivation is partly independent of—though it may of course be supported by—her explicit beliefs about

---

[6] It is a little tricky to spell out what it means for an agent to be moved by the belief that *p* unconditionally. The basic thought is that she would be moved by the belief that *p* even if she did not explicitly believe that *p* is a reason for her to act. No doubt this counterfactual formulation is in need of refinement; but I take it that the idea is clear enough.

practical reason. As Hursthouse argues, the courageous agent is moved immediately by such thoughts as "I could probably save him if I climb up there," "No one else will volunteer," "If we give in now, it will be hard to stand firm later," the temperate agent by such thoughts as: "I'm driving," "You want it more than I do," "The cheaper one will do the job," and so on (1995: 25).[7] There is no need for the further reflection that these facts provide her with reasons to act. (anti 7 oot ?)

At this point, complications crowd in. Let me begin by canceling the false impression that the ethical virtues are defined each by a list of specific dispositions, which might be characterized in terms like those in the previous paragraph. What Hursthouse gives are mere examples, not materials for defining the virtues of character. There are many different *ways* to have the canonical virtues, like justice, benevolence, and courage, which are defined not by a list of dispositional components, but by the "sphere" in which they constitute good character.[8] The sphere of courage is fear; the sphere of benevolence is other people's needs; the sphere of justice—in one sense of the term—is the distribution of limited resources. Within a given sphere, there is room for different dispositions to count as just or brave. (This fact is significant for the application of the virtue theory, as we will see below.)

A second false impression is that there is no more to the virtues of character than the sorts of disposition considered so far. I have been pressing towards a picture of ethical virtue that respects what Iris Murdoch calls "the fact that an unexamined life can be virtuous" (1970: 2).[9] If the virtuous person need not engage in explicit evaluative reflection, she need not employ a worked-out theory of reasons in deciding what to do. Ethical virtue is not primarily an intellectual power, a capacity for ethical theory, but a practical excellence one shows in one's response to the facts. This points towards a truth within "particularism": the practical

[7] Hursthouse is generalizing a proposal made by Williams (1995b: 17–18) about the non-executive virtues. They are both interested in the interpretation of Aristotle's claim (*NE* 1105a32) that the virtuous person decides on virtuous actions *for themselves*. I don't mean to say anything about that interpretive dispute.

[8] For this picture of the virtues, see Nussbaum (1988: 34–6). To say that we should think of a virtue as goodness of character in some limited "sphere" is not to imply that there is no overlap between these spheres, or that they can be fully specified without the language of the virtues in question.

[9] There is a risk that we will over-state this point, as perhaps in Murdoch's claim that goodness is "most convincingly met with in simple people—inarticulate, unselfish mothers of large families" (1970: 51–2). I worry about the impression this creates. Nothing I have argued here depends on a patronizing celebration of the "primitive," or on the association of virtue with what is inarticulate in any sense beyond the failure to articulate its own principles. Nor do I mean that a virtuous person *cannot* be articulate or philosophically reflective; the point is that she does not *need* to be.

thought involved in the virtues of character need not rely on principles, however qualified, but only on the particular considerations in virtue of which *this* rather than *that* is the thing to be done. And when reasons must be weighed, the balance is typically constituted by the dispositions that make up the virtues, not by the content of an explicit judgement. In working towards these claims, I have focused on a relatively narrow range of practical dispositions, those involved in being moved by one's beliefs. This is only a fraction of practical thought, and a smaller fraction of what our character involves.

So, for instance, it is not sufficient for being generous that one is disposed to give weight to the fact that one can help others, or please them, in certain ways; one must be apt to find opportunities for doing so. Likewise, a just person does not simply respond to injustice when it is pointed out to him; he is disposed to notice it. One aspect of virtue, then, is a kind of perception, an immediate sensitivity to the world.[10] This applies not only to facts that figure as reasons for the virtuous person, but also to *options*, to things she might do. The brave person has a sense of possibilities in action that are closed off to the coward: it is not "out of her hands"; there is something to be done; the situation is not as hopeless as that. In other cases, sensitivity works in reverse: there are options that a good person does *not* consider. An honest man does not weigh the pros and cons of theft as a way of making money when he needs to pay the bills. And it does not occur to the properly temperate person that another beer would cure the morning hangover. One way in which virtue can be unreflective is in failing even to contemplate a less than admirable act.

These remarks are still confined to dispositions of practical thought. But there are further dimensions of character. One of the most powerful and appealing conceptions of virtue is Aristotle's theory that a virtue of character is a mean between deficiency and excess.

> We can be afraid, for instance, or be confident, or have appetites, or get angry, or feel pity, and in general have pleasure or pain, both too much and too little, and in both ways not well. But having these feelings at the right times, about the right things, toward the right people, for the right end, and in the right way, is the intermediate and best condition, and this is proper to virtue. (NE 1106b19–24)

Although it is meant to apply to actions, as well, this account is most plausible, and most illuminating, as a claim about human emotion. It is a virtue of character to be neither excessively nor insufficiently disposed to anger, or pity, or sorrow, and to have these feelings "at the right times

---

[10] This is another theme of Murdoch (1970); see also McDowell (1979, §V) and Blum (1991).

[. . .] and in the right way." Even when we have them for *reasons*, how-ever, our feelings are not the products of practical thought, in the sense with which we have been concerned. Practical thought, as I intend it, must be directed at the motivation of action, intention, or desire. Our emotional proclivities are central to our character, even apart from their influence on what we do. Thus, while dispositions of practical thought always count as traits of character, the converse does not hold.

The emerging picture is this: one's character consists primarily in emo-tional dispositions, which may or may not affect one's action, and disposi-tions of practical thought. Possession of a virtue, like prudence or sympa-thy, depends on these, not because each virtue is defined by a single list of dispositions, but because it is a matter of having dispositions that count as good character in a given sphere. Thus one may be prudent partly in virtue of one's disposition to recognize and think about the long-term consequences of one's actions, or sympathetic in part because one feels distress at the suffering of others.

Before I connect these thoughts with the application of the virtue the-ory, I want to address a final complication. In writing about good charac-ter, it is natural to appeal to "the virtues"—justice, courage, temperance, and the rest. I have been happy to exploit this language, as in the previous paragraph. But it suggests a picture of human psychology that is poten-tially dubious, and which is in any case irrelevant to the project of this book. The picture is one of unified traits that range across much of what we do, their influence apparent in widely varying situations. There is, for instance, the idea of *compassion* as something that bears on one's contributions to Oxfam, as well as one's response to a crying child. Or there is the trait of *honesty*, which has to do with telling the truth, but also with not cheating on one's exams. The claim that human character works in anything like this way has recently come under attack.[11] Experi-ments in social psychology have been taken to show that most of us lack such "robust" or unified traits, ones that are "substantially resistant to contrary situational pressures in their behavioral manifestations" (Doris 1998: 506). Nor does it count against this evidence that we find it natural to appeal to the virtues (and vices) in interpreting one another. For we are disposed to ascribe such traits on insufficient grounds.[12]

This "situationist" trend is controversial even in psychology depart-ments, and its methodology has been disputed by philosophers.[13] There

---

[11] In what follows, I draw especially on Doris (1998) and Harman (1999), who rely in turn on Ross and Nisbet (1991).

[12] See Harman (1999) on the "fundamental attribution error."

[13] See, in particular, a compelling critique by Gopal Sreenivasan (2002), to which I am much indebted.

is a tendency for the work in question to ignore the commonplace with which I began, that character is only partly and imperfectly revealed in how we act. It is a crude conception of compassion that treats it as a disposition to help, in most situations, or that conceives of honesty as a disposition not to lie, cheat, or steal. But these conceptions, which ignore such things as the agent's interpretation of what is going on, and the weighing of conflicting reasons, seem to be assumed in the experiments on which social psychologists rely.[14] What they observe is, at most, that people who behave "compassionately" or "honestly" in one situation may not do so in another. They do not sufficiently examine whether the situations are different in ethically relevant respects.

I do not mean to place much weight, however, on these critical remarks about "situationism." Whatever its defects, this movement surely has a point, one that is already recognized by Plato in the *Republic*, when he depicts ordinary human character as fragmented and unstable, and by Iris Murdoch, in remarking that, "as decent people, we are usually very specialized" (1970: 97). Compassion in one's personal relations is one thing; compassion for the distant needy is another. Indeed, compassion of the first kind may fragment as well, into compassion for one's friends, for one's colleagues, for one's family. All of these things can come apart.

None of this conflicts with the virtue theory I mean to defend. It is no part of my view that unified virtues are widely shared. Nor does it follow from the social-psychological research, even on the strongest reading, that we do not have emotional dispositions, or dispositions of practical thought: "situationism allows that a suitably fine-grained inventory of local traits may provide an account of personality that is both empirically adequate and theoretically useful" (Doris 1998: 508).[15] There is no argument against our having such things as the disposition to be angry in circumstances of a given kind, or to be moved to act whenever we have a certain array of psychological states. The crucial fact, for us, is that these narrow dispositions are traits of character, in a suitably modest and unambitious sense of "trait." They are aspects or features of character, ones that can be assessed in terms of virtue and vice. Quite apart from the possibility of benevolence or justice, in general, we can ask whether a specific disposition is benevolent or just, and whether it is good or bad, as a trait of character. Judgements of this sort were involved, for instance, in the story about Marge with which I began. We can say that her disposi-

---

[14] This point is made with great clarity, and at much greater length, by Sreenivasan, who asks whether social psychologists have successfully managed to "operationalize" the traits they wish to study (2002: 57–61).

[15] See also Sreenivasan (2002: 50, 65–6).

tions are insensitive, self-serving, and unscrupulous, without having to ask whether they are confined to situations of one specific kind. So long as these judgements make sense, we have the materials we need for a virtue-theoretic interpretation of what is good in practical thought.

It only remains to say something more about the *application* of this approach. Here we need to connect our claims about good character to claims about what one should do, by way of claims about what there is *reason* to do. We can appeal to a principle worked out in the introduction to this book:

> *Reasons*: The fact that p is a reason for A to ϕ just in case A has a collection of psychological states, C, such that the disposition to be moved to ϕ by C-and-the-belief-that-p is a good disposition of practical thought, and C contains no false beliefs.

If a disposition of this kind is good as a trait of character, it follows—assuming that the virtue theory is true—that it is a good disposition of practical thought, so that it corresponds to a practical reason. Nothing I say here depends on any particular claims about the content of good character. But it is helpful to begin with a simple example. Suppose, then, that it is a good trait of character not to lie to people about things that are important to them. On the virtue theory, this would mean that the fact that something matters to you is a reason for me, or for anyone, to tell you the truth about it.

A more realistic view would be more qualified: it is a good trait of character to be deterred from lying *to some extent* by beliefs about what matters to one's audience; and perhaps only to be deterred at all if one has some other beliefs—for instance, that they won't use the information in a dangerous or immoral way. Notoriously, it is not a good trait of character to be disposed to tell the truth about the whereabouts of one's friend to the gun-toting maniac at the door, no matter how much he cares about it. Other complications are possible. So the dispositions that figure in *Reasons*, and to which the virtue theory applies, may be quite intricate indeed.

The example of lying raises a further question, about conflicting reasons. It is a familiar quandary to have to weigh the fact that something is a lie against the fact that the truth will hurt. Even if both considerations are reasons for action, they have to be compared. Here, too, we can appeal to a principle worked out in the introduction:

> Reasons correspond to collections of psychological states that fuel good practical thought. One reason is *stronger* than another just in case it is a good disposition of practical thought to be *more strongly moved* by the collection of states that corresponds to it, than by the collection that corresponds to the other.

In this formula, as in *Reasons*, "good disposition" means "better than the alternative," not "fine" or "good enough." We would otherwise permit the impossible case in which two reasons are stronger than each other, because the corresponding and conflicting dispositions are both "good enough." According to the virtue theory, the question to be asked in our example is whether the disposition to be more strongly moved by the fact of lying is better, as a trait of character, than the disposition to be more strongly moved by the fact that someone's feelings will be hurt. This will presumably depend on the other features of one's circumstance: on who the person is, how badly they will react, how important the question is. As before, the dispositions that matter here will be more intricate and more qualified than my simple description suggests.

It is also simplistic to assume that, when dispositions of practical thought conflict, there will always be one that is better, as a trait of character, than the other. This might fail to happen for several reasons. If it is possible for certain virtues to be incompatible—for instance, if compassion and honesty simply collide in a given case—we may not be able to say which disposition is better. But even if that is not so, and the virtues of character can always be combined, they can be realized in many different ways. This follows from the fact, remarked above, that virtues like justice and courage are not defined by a list of specific dispositions, but by the sphere in which they constitute good character. There is room for differences of ethical "style," so that, in a given circumstance, several dispositions of practical thought may be, as traits of character, more or less equally good.[16] The virtue theory can accommodate this. What it creates is the possibility of *incomparable reasons*.

When conflicting dispositions are equally good, as traits of character, it follows from the principle above that the reasons that correspond to them cannot be balanced against one another. If it is no better to be more concerned about dishonesty than about hurt feelings, or the reverse, then neither reason will outweigh the other. (Remember that a "good disposition" here is better than the alternative, not merely "good enough.") Nor should we say that the reasons are equally strong, since that would correspond to the claim that the best disposition is one that gives them *equal* weight—and that need not be so. If none of these dispositions is better than the others, as a trait of character, the reasons in question will be incomparable: not equally good, but also not such that one is stronger than the other.[17] And so there may be, in the circumstance, no determinate answer to the question, "What should I do?" (These remarks about the

---

[16] Here I am returning, at last, to a complication raised in the second paragraph of the introduction, about the many different ways of being good.

[17] For discussion of this idea, see the collection edited by Ruth Chang (1997).

diversity of ethical virtue also make room for considerations that are not *good* reasons—since the disposition to be moved by them is no better than the alternative—but which are not *bad* reasons, either.)

It is important not to exaggerate the extent of indeterminacy here. In the case of conflict I have gestured towards, there will be a wealth of determinate facts about what I should not do: things no set of virtuous dispositions would lead me to do. And in many cases, it will be true that there is only one permissible path. But I think it is essentially a virtue of the present account that it accommodates the diversity of good character, and through it explains the possibility of incomparable reasons.

This reference to explanation—and, more generally, my account of the application of the virtue theory—could be misleading. It should not be taken to imply that facts about good character are metaphysically or epistemically prior to facts about reasons to act. To repeat a point I have made before, the virtue theory is a doctrine of reciprocity, not priority. I do not mean to recommend the epistemic strategy of settling questions about what there is reason to do by appeal to independent convictions about virtue of character. My claim is rather that, according to the virtue theory, our beliefs about reason and virtue must be brought into line. This is consistent with arguments that run in either direction—from reasons to good character, and from ethical virtue to what there is reason to do. I return to this in the conclusion of the book. Before I do so, I mean to argue that the virtue theory is true.

2. AN ARGUMENT FOR THE VIRTUE THEORY

According to the virtue theory of practical reason, being good as a disposition of practical thought is being a disposition of practical thought that is good as a trait of character. This way of putting things depends on the somewhat awkward locution, "good as." The point of this phrase is to emphasize that "good" is being used here as what Peter Geach (in "Good and Evil") has called an "attributive adjective." He explains this concept as follows:

> I shall say that in a phrase 'an A B' ('A' being an adjective and 'B' being a noun) 'A' is a (logically) predicative adjective if the predication 'is an A B' splits up logically into a pair of predications 'is a B' and 'is A'; otherwise I shall say that 'A' is a (logically) attributive adjective. (Geach 1956: 64)

Geach claims that "good" is always attributive, and has no predicative use. There is no such thing as being good *simpliciter*.

Geach is wrong, I think, to suppose that every use of "good" can be supplied with a nominal expression that determines what a thing is being evaluated *as*. This claim struggles with talk of what is good for a person and of a tool or instrument's being good for a purpose or good for doing something.[18] But he is right to observe that "good" makes no sense on its own: we have to be told *how* a thing is being evaluated, even if it is simply "as a state of affairs," or "as good for me." And he is right to argue that one way in which this is done is by supplying a term for the relevant *kind*—in a suitably unambitious sense of "kind." (In particular, we need not appeal to a natural kind, or a kind of artifact; and something may belong to several kinds at once.) In many cases, the kind is specified by the noun phrase that follows "good"; but we should not insist on this. The *context* may help to determine what kind of thing an object is being evaluated as (Geach 1956: 65–6). When this is so, we can always fill out the missing contextual material, so as to say, more precisely, that it is being evaluated *as an F* or *as a G*.

In what follows, I adopt the terminology of "Good and Evil," transposed from the formal to the material mode. When I say that *good* is *attributive*, I mean three things: first, that for some kinds, at least, things can be evaluated *as* members of that kind; second, that being a good F (or good *as an F*) is *not* just a matter of being an F and being *good*; third, that the standards for being a good F may differ from the standards for being a good G, even when Fs are a kind of G. We can illustrate the last two points with a familiar example: being a good theft is not a matter of being a theft and being good; and the standards for being a good theft are not the standards for being a good act, even though theft is a kind of act.

The claims in the previous paragraph articulate a minimal, logical sense for the principle that *good* is attributive. They correspond closely to the arguments given by Geach (1956: 64), except that they do not imply, as Geach apparently does, that *good* must *always* attach to a relevant kind. (See the remarks about "good for," above.) Understood in this qualified way, the claim that *good* is attributive seems to me quite evidently correct.

Unfortunately, Geach has come to be associated with more ambitious and more dubious views. It is therefore crucial to insist that, when I say that *good* is attributive, what I have in mind is nothing more than the logical point expressed above. This point does not imply that the standards for being a good F can always be deduced from analytic or conceptual truths about what it is to be an F. That view is attributed to Geach by R. M. Hare, in an influential article: "[Geach] thinks that [. . .] the meaning of the word 'good,' taken in conjunction with that of the word

---

[18] For discussion of the varied ways in which things can be good, see Thomson (1992) and Szabó (2001, sections 3 and 4). Szabó denies that "good" works as a "predicate-modifier" in general, but he allows that there is such a thing as evaluating something *as an F.* That is sufficient for the claims I go on to make.

'knife' or that of the word 'stomach,' enables us to specify the traits which things of these kinds have to have in order to be called 'good' " (1957: 78). But this is not a consequence of the claim that *good* is attributive, understood in the logical sense; it is quite implausible; and I cannot see that it corresponds to anything in "Good and Evil."[19] Nor does it follow that no sense can be made of the claim that *x* is a good *thing*, a good *event*, or a good *state of affairs*. It *may* be true, as Geach (1956: 71–2) insists, that "we cannot sensibly speak of a good or bad event, a good or bad thing to happen," but that is not a consequence of the principle that *good* is attributive, taken on its own. It says nothing about which kinds generate standards for being good, or how they are generated.

Among the kinds for which there *do* seem to be such standards are the ones that matter to the virtue theory of practical reason: dispositions of practical thought and traits of character. It is the fact that *good* is attributive, in the logical sense, that makes the virtue theory of practical reason a substantive claim. The standards for being a good disposition of practical thought might differ from the standards for being a good trait of character, even though, as I argued in section 1, dispositions of practical thought are traits of character. In this way, there is at least a nominal distinction to be drawn between practical reason and ethical virtue. In order to argue for the virtue theory, one would have to show that this nominal distinction does not correspond to anything real: it is a distinction without a difference. That is what I propose to do.[20] In the rest of this section, I argue, from the metaphysics of *being good*, that it is only if one adopts a rationalist conception of practical reason that one can distinguish its standards from the standards of good character, applied to practical thought. The focus then will turn to the prospects for ethical rationalism. As I argue in the remainder of the book, these prospects are bleak.

[19] Geach (1956: 69) does say that, if I do not know what hygrometers are for, I do not what "hygrometer" means, and so I do not know what "good hygrometer" means, and that, if the phrase is to make sense, the *A* in 'good *A*' must "convey [. . .] a standard of goodness" (1956: 71). But these claims are much weaker than the doctrine of "deduction from the concept" ascribed to him by Hare.

[20] The need for further argument here is apparently missed by Philippa Foot:

Now, in describing virtues in terms of (a) the recognition of particular considerations as reasons for acting, and (b) the relevant action, I have only been expressing familiar and time-honoured ideas of moral goodness. But how can it be denied that I have at the same time been talking about practical rationality? The discussion has been about human goodness in respect of reason-recognition and reason-following, and if this is not practical rationality I should like to know what is. (Foot, 2001: 13)

Foot's equation of virtue and practical reason will seem deniable to those who acknowledge the attributive character of *good*.

In defending as innocuous the claim that *good* is attributive, I rejected the implausible suggestion (due to Hare, as a reading of Geach) that the standards for being a good *F* can always be deduced from analytic or conceptual truths about what it is to be an *F*. Even if there are concepts that permit such deduction—ones that describe things in terms of highly specific functions or ends (Foot 1961: 134–6)—it is not generally the case. For instance, a concept might pick out a kind of thing that has a definite function, without the concept including a specification of the function, as when we name an organ whose role in the organism is only later discovered (Foot 1961: 138). In another case, the specification of the function or end that figures in the concept may be too spare to admit of any comprehensive deduction of the standards of goodness. (Even if it is analytic that the heart is an organ whose function is to pump blood, that tells us very little about what it is to pump blood well, or what it is for a heart to be good: we know that a heart that cannot pump blood is defective, but not much more.) And in a third sort of case, we may be hard pressed to specify any function or characteristic end at all, even though we are competent with the concept of an *F*. Here we might think of concepts like *person*, *action*, or *event*.

The final difficulty is one basis of the view, also mentioned above, that it makes no sense to speak of a good event. And it leads some critics of the claim that *good* is attributive to argue that, since it does make sense to speak of a good person, and since the concept of a person fails to specify a function or characteristic end, this must be a non-attributive use of "good."[21] Both of these arguments are flawed: the first because it relies on the misguided doctrine of "deduction from the concept"; the second because it conflates that controversial doctrine with the innocuous claim that *good* is attributive, in the logical sense.

Still the idea of "deduction from the concept" has a residual appeal. It is, I think, the psychologized version of a metaphysical truth, that the standards for being a good *F* are determined by the *nature* of *F*s, as such. If it makes sense to speak about good *F*s at all, then *F*s must have a common character that serves to fix the criteria of goodness for things of that kind.[22] Such rhetoric is notoriously obscure, in part because the idea of "determining" is so difficult to understand. My contention will be relatively weak: there is a sense in which the standards of goodness as an *F* supervene intelligibly on the nature of *F*s.

Imagine a continuum of metaphysical dependence claims. At one extreme, there is the analogue of "deduction from the concept": where it

---

[21] For an exemplary expression of the latter tendency, see Pigden (1990).

[22] Compare Geach (1956: 71). For a compelling rehabilitation of talk about the *natures* of things, see Fine (1994).

makes sense to speak of a good *F*, complete grasp of the nature of *Fs* *would* permit us to deduce the standards for being a good *F*. At the other extreme, there is a trivial form of supervenience: no difference in standards without a difference in kinds. If being an *F* just *is* being a *G* then the standards for being a good *F* are exactly the standards for being a good *G*.[23] The claim I have in mind falls sensibly between these two extremes.

> *The Difference Principle*: If *Fs* are a kind of *G*, and being a *good F* is not simply a matter of being an *F* that is a *good G*, there must be something in the distinctive nature of *Fs* to explain or illuminate the difference.

To take, once again, the most familiar example, the standards for being a good theft are not the standards for being a good action; and we can say something about the *nature* of theft to explain the difference. A theft is, *inter alia*, the dishonest appropriation of another's property with the end of making it one's own. When we evaluate a theft, as such, we ask how well it achieves the aims that belong to the nature of theft: does the thief make off with the loot, in his safe and secure possession? Without claiming that the standards of good theft can be deduced from the metaphysics of theft—still less from my rough specification of what theft is—we can see how the nature of theft introduces an evaluative standard that is foreign to the evaluation of action in general.

The demand for a *relevant* difference cannot always be met. Adopting an idea from Parfit, someone might employ special and unusual standards in the evaluation of thefts-on-Tuesdays (1984: 124). But even if we grant that it makes sense to speak of a nature here, so that we are dealing with two *kinds*—thefts and thefts-on-Tuesdays—one included in the other, it is clear that the difference between them could not ground a difference in evaluative standards. There is nothing in the property of occurring on Tuesday that could serve to introduce a new standard of evaluation for thefts. If *Fs* are a kind of *G*, and being a good *F* is not simply a matter of being an *F* that is a good *G*, there must be something in the distinctive nature of *Fs* to *explain* or *illuminate* the difference.

The explanation need not be as simple as the one that applies to theft. So, for instance, the standards for being a good crime are not the standards for being a good thing to do, but it would be a mistake to speak of the aim or end of crime, as such. What we can say is that a good crime is a good instance of some particular kind of crime—theft, arson, fraud, and

---

[23] This claim suggests a simple argument for the virtue theory of practical reason. If being a trait of character just *is* being a disposition of practical thought, then being good in one way is the same as being good in the other. Unfortunately, as we saw in section 1, the premise of this argument is false. There are traits of character—for instance, certain kinds of emotional disposition—that do not bear on practical thought.

so on—where the natures of particular crimes can be seen to introduce distinctive standards of evaluation. *Crime* stands as a determinable to these determinates, and that structure is in this case sufficient for the kind of explanation that the Difference Principle demands.

Although I have used examples that are kinds of *action*, where it is natural to speak of an "aim" or "end," the Difference Principle applies more generally. Thus it can be argued that there are distinctive standards for being a good parent, or a good teacher, that are not simply standards for being a good person. They turn on the distinctive *role* of parents and teachers, among people in general. By contrast, it does *not* make sense to suppose that there are distinctive standards for being a good person-with-blue-eyes, because there is nothing in the colour of one's eyes from which these standards could derive.

The same point can be made in a context closer to the one that will interest us below: the evaluation of *thought*. It is because practical thought involves intention and desire, not just belief, that there is a distinction between practical and theoretical reason. As Anscombe says, "[t]here is a difference of form between reasoning leading to action and reasoning for the truth of a conclusion" (1963: 60). That is why different standards apply to them. At the very least, since *akrasia* is possible, practical reason cannot simply be conceived as theoretical reason, applied to questions of how one should live; there must be a non-theoretical standard of acting as one thinks one should. (As I will argue in section 3, even this concession is not enough; the difference between practical and theoretical reason is deeper than it suggests.) On the other hand, it is clear that the standards of thought that apply to the history or geography of different countries must be the same, because there is nothing in *that* difference of subject-matter to explain how they could diverge.

I have to admit that I do not know how to articulate the sense of explanation at work here, except by giving examples like these. The intuition is that a difference in evaluative standards for two different kinds, one of which belongs within the other, must be grounded in a *relevant* difference between the nature of those kinds. If a certain kind of action, like theft, is evaluatively distinctive, it must be *metaphysically* distinctive, in a way that explains why it has the standards it does. If a certain kind of thought is subject to distinctive standards, they must derive from the kind of thought it is.

This point is the basis of an argument for the virtue theory of practical reason. It is a consequence of the Difference Principle, together with the fact that dispositions of practical thought are traits of character, that if the virtue theory is false—if being a good disposition of practical thought is not simply a matter of being a disposition of practical thought that is a good trait of character—there must be something about the nature of practical thought to explain or illuminate its failure. Dispositions of practical thought must be distinctive, as traits of character, in a way that explains why they are subject to their own evaluative standard. If there is nothing in the nature of practical thought to indicate this standard, something distinct from the standard of good character, the virtue theory must be true. As I will argue later on, there is *nothing* about our dispositions of practical thought that could ground the difference in evaluative standards that the virtue theorist denies.

What I am developing here is the crucial lemma announced above: that *ethical rationalism* is the only alternative to the virtue theory of practical reason. By "rationalism," I mean the attempt to explain why practical thought has the standards it does by appeal to its distinctive character—to derive the standards of practical reason, in outline, from the nature of practical thought. In other words, I mean precisely the kind of view that would meet the challenge posed by Difference Principle. We can usefully think of this as a watered-down version of the "constitutive aim" approach to practical reason. The constitutive aim theorist begins with an account of what it is to act for reasons, and thus with a partial account of practical thought. His idea is that, along with the particular goals we have in acting in particular ways, our action counts as being done for reasons in virtue of having a distinctive goal: the "constitutive aim" of action. To act for reasons is to act in a way that aims at the satisfaction of desire; or it is to act for the sake of the good; or in a way that will achieve self-knowledge; or reflective endorsement of oneself and what one does.[24] Whatever its content, the constitutive aim of action need not be an *explicit* goal that the agent has; it may simply be a matter of the mechanisms by which intentional action is "constitutively regulated," a tendency that operates within us as an essential part of acting for reasons, whether we know it or not.[25] The pivotal claim of the constitutive aim theory is that one acts *well*—one meets the standards of practical reason—just to the extent that one achieves the constitutive aim of action. Action is like theft: it has an end of its own, one that determines whether it is good or bad, as such. The standards of practical reason can thus be derived from the metaphysics of acting for a reason, and the Difference Principle can be met.

The constitutive aim approach is a version of rationalism, in my sense of the word, but an especially ambitious one. It aims for a full account of

---

[24] For the first claim, about desire, see Williams (1980) and Dreier (1997); for the achievement of "the good," see Bond (1983: 30–1), Railton (1997: 62–4), and Wedgwood (2003); on action and self-knowledge, see Velleman (1989; 2000b); and on reflective endorsement, see Korsgaard (1996). These views are discussed in more detail below.

[25] This point is stressed by Velleman (2000b: 19–21).

practical reason, not just a sketch of what is distinctive about it; and it appeals to the nature of *action*, in particular, not to practical thought in general. In these respects it goes beyond what is required to satisfy the Difference Principle and block the argument for the virtue theory. All we need for that is an account of practical thought that helps to explain why it is subject to evaluative standards of its own. We need not restrict ourselves to the metaphysics of action; we need not find an "aim" in any ordinary sense; and we need not hope for a full account of the standards of practical thought. Unlike the constitutive aim theorist, properly so-called, the rationalist sets the bar of explanation relatively low.

Still the demand for explanation is substantive. According to the Difference Principle, divergence of standards always depends on, and derives from, the nature of the kinds to which those standards are applied. It follows that an answer to the Difference Principle must belong to *moral psychology*. It must say what is special about dispositions of practical thought, among our traits of character—*why* they are subject to a standard of their own, and, roughly, what it is.

In effect, I am arguing that Anscombe was right when she said that we cannot do moral philosophy without an "adequate philosophy of psychology" (Anscombe 1958: 26). What we need, at least, is an account of practical thought on which we can see whether the Difference Principle is satisfied. If we cannot derive the standards of practical reason, at least in outline, from the nature of practical thought—if ethical rationalism is a mistake—then the virtue theory wins by default: a disposition of practical thought is good, as such, just in case it is good as a trait of character. In what follows, I argue for the antecedent of this conditional. The right account of practical thought is one on which the Difference Principle cannot be satisfied. Ethical rationalism is false.

3. PRACTICAL REASON AND THE GUISE OF THE GOOD

The purpose of this section is to explore some connections between rationalism in ethics and the action-theoretic doctrine of the guise of the good. I rely on the arguments of Part One to criticize both "recognitional" and "Kantian constructivist" accounts of reason in action. For all their differences, I am interested in what these theories have in common. I end by exploring the prospects for constructivism or non-recognitional rationalism, without the guise of the good.

According to the recognitional view, practical thought is principally thought *about* good reasons, as such. "Practical deliberation [. . .] is *reasoning about what is best (or satisfactory) to do with a view to making up one's mind about what to do*" (Watson 2003: 175).

Some care is necessary here. The claim that practical thought is about what there is reason to do must not be confused with the platitude, described in the introduction, that *good* practical thought is responsive to reasons (except in the case of false belief). This platitude does nothing to respond to the Difference Principle. It does nothing to show that the property of being good as a disposition of practical thought, applied to dispositions of the appropriate kind, is different from the property of being good as a trait of character. It is effectively silent about the *content* of responsiveness to reasons. By contrast, the recognitional view does appear to satisfy the Difference Principle. Dispositions of practical thought are dispositions to form and revise beliefs about what there is reason to do, and to be moved by those beliefs. It follows that they are subject to distinctive standards of their own. One standard is concerned with *akrasia*, the failure to act on one's beliefs. The other standard is *epistemic*: it is concerned with forming correct, or reasonable, beliefs. Practical reason is a matter of thinking well about what one should do, and of acting as one thinks one should.[26]

The claim is not, of course, that we can determine what there is reason to do just from the claim that practical thought involves beliefs about what there is reason to do. There is no prospect of that. It is rather that dispositions of practical thought are subject to standards of their own because they depend on such beliefs. These standards do not apply to traits of character in general: they *can* apply only to dispositions that involve beliefs about practical reason. It makes no sense to apply the epistemic standard of thinking well about what one should do, or the standard of acting as one thinks one should, to dispositions that do not involve the relevant beliefs. According to the recognitional view, this is what is special about dispositions of practical thought, why they are subject to a standard apart from the standard of good character, and how the Difference Principle is met.[27]

---

[26] For views of this kind, see Cullity and Gaut (1997: 4–5) and Wedgwood (2003: 206–7); they correspond to the "High Brow" conception of Railton (1997: 62–4).

[27] It is worth asking, in light of the Difference Principle, whether we can make the distinction between *ethics* and *epistemology* required by the recognitional view. After all, our ethical and epistemic dispositions, our traits of character and the tendencies involved when we form and revise beliefs, belong to the general category of psychological traits. Are we forced to think in terms of single evaluative property—being good as a psychological trait—applied to different sorts of disposition? Is there no more fundamental contrast between ethical and intellectual virtue? I think there *is* a difference here, as there seems to be. This difference flows from the fact that epistemic dispositions are ones in which we form and revise *beliefs*, and from the fact that *truth* is the standard of correctness for belief. That is why the epistemic and ethical evaluation of thought can come apart. (Example: optimism may be good as a trait of character, but if, as many claim, it involves an over-estimation of oneself, that could make it epistemically bad.) It is very difficult to make this point with more precision. Everyone should agree that epistemic standards have *something* to do with the fact that beliefs are correct if true, and incorrect otherwise. But we must resist a crude reliabilism,

I have so far described a version of the recognitional view on which the subject-matter of practical thought is practical reason itself. But we can obviously generalize. If Aristotle believes that the topic of deliberation is happiness or the human good, and that practical wisdom is therefore best conceived as motivating knowledge of the good, then he is a kind of recognitional rationalist.[28] In saying this, he need not deny the equivalence of practical reason and ethical virtue, but he does imply that there are distinct properties here: being good as a disposition of practical thought and being good as a trait of character. It is then the task of an argument— perhaps an argument about the reciprocity of the ethical virtues (*NE* 1144b31–1145a2)—to show that they fall into line. On the virtue theory of practical reason, as I intend it, there is no need for that further argument, since the properties in question cannot be distinguished at all.

Whatever form it takes, the recognitional approach is subject to a decisive problem: it relies on the claim that practical thought takes place under the guise of the good, if not in exactly the form rejected in Part One, then in something close enough to be discredited by the same arguments. Practical reason is the subject-matter of *explicit* practical thought, which is therefore subject to the epistemic standards that govern belief. But if the arguments of Part One are right, it is not the topic of practical thought in general. We can be moved by reasons, and act on them, without the belief that those reasons are good. It follows that the standard of thinking well about what one should do and acting on one's beliefs cannot apply to practical thought, as such. So it cannot be identified with the standard of practical reason, which must apply to dispositions that involve no such beliefs. At most, it is a fragment of practical reason—and not a fundamental one. For it is parasitic on the facts about what there is reason to do, which are equivalent, by *Reasons*, to facts about good dispositions of practical thought, dispositions that need not involve beliefs about practical reason. The standards that apply to these dispositions are more basic than the standards that apply to explicit practical thought.

on which epistemically good dispositions are simply those that deliver the truth. In general, it is not clear how the content of epistemology could be derived, in detail, from the constitutive aim of belief. (For connections between epistemology and the aim of belief, see Velleman 1996: 184–5; 2000a; 2000b: 17–18; Railton 1997; Korsgaard 1997: 249; and Wedgwood 2002.) I am afraid that we must leave these matters dark. What we need, in order to make sense of the recognitional view, is the vague but plausible claim that epistemic standards are distinctive, among the standards of good psychology, because they depend on the connection between truth and belief.

[28] For the role of the apparent good in deliberation, see *NE* 1113a15–34; for practical wisdom as knowledge of the good, see *NE* 1140b5, 1140b22, 1141b13–14, and 1142b34. Warren Quinn defends an Aristotelian version of the recognitional view, on which "practical rationality chiefly consists in correctness of thought about human good and evil" (1993: 253).

The problem is much the same for other versions of the recognitional view, like those which appeal to beliefs about happiness or the human good. Beliefs of this kind are *sometimes* involved in practical thought. But if it is wrong to say that we act under the guise of the good, in the sense explored in Part One, it is even more implausible to say that we act "under the guise of happiness": that we aim at happiness or the human good in everything we do. The sufficient conditions of acting for a reason, or being moved by one, do not depend on evaluative beliefs of any kind. So practical reason cannot simply be a matter of thinking well about some evaluative subject-matter, and of acting on one's beliefs. The standards of practical reason must apply to dispositions that involve no such beliefs. This is not to deny that there *are* evaluative facts, and facts about practical reason, in particular. It is not a rejection of "realism," in any ordinary sense. What is at stake here is an explanatory claim. If there is a difference between being good as a disposition of practical thought and being good as a trait of character, it cannot derive from the recognitional content of practical thought.

It is often assumed, at this point, that *constructivism* is the only non-sceptical alternative to the recognitional approach. They are introduced as opposing views that, together with scepticism about practical reason, exhaust the whole of logical space.[29] In the context of the virtue theory and the Difference Principle, this ought to look like a mistake. For the constructivist, the standards of practical reason can be derived from an account of practical thought that does not rely on its being sensitive to the evaluative facts. It appeals instead to formal features of the concepts it deploys, to the role of rational dispositions or desire in motivation, or to the fact that, in acting for reasons, we know what we are doing and why. Apart from its high ambition—to fix, in detail, the content of practical reason—this is equivalent in my terms to *non-recognitional rationalism*. In other words, the dispute between constructivist and recognitional views is a dispute between different forms of ethical rationalism. They agree that the standards of practical reason must derive from the nature of practical thought, but they disagree on how. (Does the derivation appeal to the epistemology of evaluative belief?) We need not accept their shared assumption: we can reject constructivism *and* the recognitional view by giving up on ethical rationalism. If we do so, the consequence is not scepticism, but, as we saw in the argument of section 2, the virtue theory of practical reason.

[29] This framework is made explicit in the introduction to *Ethics and Practical Reason*, a collection that has had a powerful influence on the present debate (Cullity and Gaut, eds., 1997). See also Wedgwood (2003: 206–7).

The framework that makes this option invisible, by treating constructivism and the recognitional view as the only non-sceptical possibilities, derives in part from the influence of John Rawls. In the third lecture of "Kantian Constructivism in Moral Theory," he contrasts his Kantian approach with a "rational intuitionism" he finds in Samuel Clarke and Richard Price, Henry Sidgwick, and W. D. Ross. It is clear that his division is not exhaustive, and is not meant to be. So, for instance, the rational intuitionist holds a specific sort of recognitional view, one on which moral concepts are irreducible, and moral truths self-evident (Rawls 1980: 343–4). And *Kantian* constructivism may be contrasted with the kind of *instrumentalism* that takes a constructivist form. Still, it is tempting to suppose, as others have done, that we can generalize from here: that we can find a distinction in Rawls that will apply to any possible view.

I think this is the origin of Korsgaard's difficult remarks about "substantive" and "procedural" realism in *The Sources of Normativity*. The substantive realist is characterized in several ways: as someone who "insists on the irreducible character of normativity" (1996: 32), who "declares that some things are *intrinsically* normative" (1996: 33), and who "conceives ethics as a branch of knowledge, knowledge of the normative part of the world" (1996: 37). The point about irreducibility is complicated by the fact that reductive naturalism turns out to be a form of substantive realism (1996: 40). What unifies the forms of non-reductive and reductive realism that Korsgaard counts as *substantive* is, I think, something like allegiance to a recognitional conception of practical reason. Or since her topic is morality in particular, "[substantive] moral realism is the view that there are answers to moral questions *because* there are moral facts or truths, which those questions ask *about*" (1996: 35). *Procedural* realism is introduced as the view that answers to moral questions, or questions of practical reason, are possible, but do not have the kind of ground that the substantive realist claims. This is, on the face of it, nothing more than the joint rejection of scepticism and the recognitional view. As the name suggests, however, Korsgaard assumes that procedural realism will be *constructivist*: in one way or another, it will derive the standards of moral judgement—or, in our case, of practical reason—from the process of moral, or practical, thought.[30] If we want to keep in view the possibility of the virtue theory, we have to remember that constructivism is *not* the only alternative to scepticism and the recognitional view. When matters

---

[30] This is clear in the examples with which she illustrates procedural realism (Korsgaard 1996: 35–6), in her treatment of "dogmatic rationalism" in "The Normativity of Instrumental Reason" (Korsgaard 1997: 239–243), and in the conceptions of practical reason she defends.

are presented in that way, it is because the truth of a substantive doctrine—what I have called "ethical rationalism"—is simply being assumed.

I have argued against the recognitional rationalist on grounds that may be congenial to Korsgaard and to Rawls. Like me, they are critical of the moral psychology of the recognitional view, a picture of practical thought that makes it too theoretical, too much a matter of tracking the evaluative facts.[31] Perhaps ironically, I want to criticize the Kantian constructivist on very similar grounds. The problem with the recognitional view, on my account, is not that it conceives the facts about practical reason as "intrinsically normative," or that it relies on "heteronomy of the will" (Kant 1785, 4: 441), but that its appeal to evaluative belief in practical thought is a version of the guise of the good. I find the same mistake at work in the argument of Kant's *Groundwork*, and in Korsgaard's development and revision of that argument in *The Sources of Normativity*.

The crucial point is this: when Kant purports to derive the content of the moral law, as a categorical imperative, from his theory of the will, he assumes that a rational agent is one who aims to justify what she does. When we picture the "rational being" of *Groundwork III*, choosing how to act "under the idea of freedom"—as though completely unconstrained by inclination—we are meant to picture an appeal to *reasons* that do not depend on inclination in any way. Since they do not depend on inclination, these reasons are categorical. So, as rational beings, we are committed to acting in conformity with categorical reasons, and according to the argument of *Groundwork II*, we are thus committed to the substance of the moral law. Insofar as we act "under the idea of freedom," we are committed to choosing maxims we can will as universal laws, and to respecting humanity, in ourselves and others, as an end in itself. Since these dispositions belong to rational agents, just as such, they correspond to the content of a categorical imperative.

This argument has been criticized at every step: for assuming a kind of transcendental freedom; for leaving a gap between commitment to categorical reasons and to the formula of universal law; for taking this, mistakenly, to be equivalent to the formula of humanity; and on the ground that Kant's expression of the moral law is an "empty formalism." The problem I have in mind turns on a feature of Kant's account to which his critics are often sympathetic: the claim that, in acting for a reason, a ratio-

---

[31] See Rawls (1980: 345–6), and Korsgaard (1996: 44–7; 1997: 239–243). Korsgaard argues that the "dogmatic" or recognitional rationalist cannot give a properly "reciprocal account of rationality—as some sort of human function or capacity—and of reasons" (1997: 243). This is presumably because, in doing so, he is forced to conceive of "rationality"—which means, in this context, the power of practical thought—as the capacity to track the evaluative facts. As Korsgaard argues, that conception is a mistake.

nal being must take herself to have good reason to act. This claim conflicts with the argument of Part One. Whatever is involved in taking oneself to have good reason for what one does—a commitment to will one's maxim as a universal law, or to treat humanity as an end—one need not do so in order to act for reasons, or to engage in practical thought. That is why there is no prospect of meeting the Difference Principle along the lines of *Groundwork III*. As a form of rationalism, Kant's argument about the reciprocity of freedom and the moral law is subject to the same objection as the recognitional view: it depends on the bad assumption that, in acting for reasons, we act under the guise of the good.[32]

This problem survives in Korsgaard's subtle re-conception of the Kantian approach. Her argument begins with the idea that intentional action is essentially *reflective*, so that the standards of practical reason are standards of reflective success (Korsgaard 1996: 92–4). This depends on the adoption of a "practical identity": "a description under which you find your life to be worth living and your actions to be worth undertaking" (1996: 101). As for Kant, the task of reflection is to find the "unconditioned": "we should never stop reflecting until we have reached a satisfactory answer, one that admits of no further questioning" (1996: 258). The consequence is supposed to be that, in order to be fully reflective, and thus to meet the standards of practical reason, we must value our own humanity—our reflective nature—and thus the humanity of others. In Korsgaard's provocative statement, "It follows that human beings are valuable. Enlightenment morality is true" (1996: 123).

As with the argument of the *Groundwork*, there are many points at which we might resist—though Korsgaard is sensitive to most of them. She is careful to distinguish a modest form of categorical imperative from the content of the moral law (1996: 97–100), and to argue at length, in Lecture Four, that we cannot respect our own humanity without respecting the same feature in everyone else. She is also more explicit about the conditions of reflection in acting for reasons:

> [We] human animals turn our attention on to our perceptions and desires themselves, on to our own mental activities, and we are conscious *of* them. That is why we can think *about* them. [. . .] And this sets us a problem no other animal has. [. . .] For our capacity to turn our attention on to our own mental activities is also a capacity to distance ourselves from them, and to call them into question. [. . .] Shall I act? Is this desire really a *reason* to act? The reflective mind

---

[32] In thinking about the structure of Kant's argument, I have been helped by Allison (1986). It is explicit in his account that Kant relies on a version of the guise of the good (see Allison 1986: 405–6).

cannot settle for perception and desire, not just as such. It needs a *reason*. Otherwise, at least as long as it reflects, it cannot commit itself, or go forward. (Korsgaard 1996: 93)

The conclusion of this passage may seem conditional—"as long as it reflects"—but really it is not. The claim is that "being human[,] we must endorse our impulses before we can act on them" (1996: 122). This amounts to something like a non-cognitive version of the guise of the good: taking something as a reason is a matter of *reflective endorsement*, or of the fact that one *values* oneself under a practical identity that demands a certain response.

Once again, the Kantian project is vulnerable to the arguments given in Part One. Those arguments do not depend on whether the judgement that something is a normative reason is understood in cognitive or non-cognitive terms. In acting for a reason, one takes something as one's reason to act in an *explanatory*, not a normative sense. One need not believe that it is a good reason to act; one need not endorse one's response to it; and one need not value oneself as the kind of person who has that response.

One virtue of Korsgaard's discussion is that she does not simply take for granted her version of the guise of the good. She thinks of it as something that follows from the "reflective structure of human consciousness" (1996: 113), as in the argument of the passage quoted above. But it is a moral of the Part One theory of intentional action that this sort of argument rests on a mistake, that of conflating reflection as *reflexivity*—as in the knowledge of what one is doing and why—with reflection as evaluative thought.[33] Korsgaard is right to say that, in acting for a reason, one takes something as one's reason to act. I have argued that this is a matter of desire-like belief about the explanation of one's action; this is the sense in which we *choose* what our reasons will be. It does not follow that we choose to act for reasons we endorse, or think of as good.

These arguments against the Kantian constructivist may seem too quick. If that is so, it is partly because the work of refuting the guise of the good was finished by the end of Part One. All that remains is to locate that doctrine in the Kantian argument. It is also because the guise of the good is something that figures deep in the strategy that Kant and Korsgaard share, a strategy that appeals to the commitments we assume when we deploy the concept of justification in acting for reasons. If this depends on a false conception of acting for reasons, the constructivist argument

---

[33] I made the same point, in connection with Korsgaard (1997), at the beginning of Part One, section 6.

will fail on grounds that have little or nothing to do with its most interest-ing parts—the idea of a practical identity, in Korsgaard, or of universal law, in Kant.

This may suggest a limited retreat: if they work, these Kantian argu-ments at least apply to those who *do* care about acting for good reasons. They show, for instance, that if one aims to justify one's actions, one is committed to the value of humanity as an end in itself. I am sceptical about this; but I do not need to dispute it here. Without the guise of the good, claims about what is involved in taking oneself to have good reason to act do not speak to the project of *rationalism*; they make no contact with the nature of practical thought, as such. So they do nothing to contest the argument for the virtue theory proposed in section 2.

There is, in any case, a more promising way to rescue the Kantian idea: we can try for a kind of constructivism that does not assume that we must act for reasons we regard as good. Having explained the structure of this approach, below, I will argue for two further claims: first, that it corre-sponds to a certain kind of *internalism* about practical reason; and sec-ond, that we should be suspicious of internalism, of the sort at issue here, on action-theoretic grounds.

One way to think about the new constructivist strategy is that it turns from the *form* of practical thought to conditions that govern its *content*. Suppose that the capacity for practical thought depends on having spe-cific dispositions, without which it would not be possible. It turns out, for instance, that in order to act for reasons one must be disposed to give weight to a certain class of considerations—about one's own desires, or others' welfare, or whatever. This would be the kind of fact that would meet the Difference Principle; it would explain why practical thought is subject to a distinctive standard. If practical thought is by nature the exercise of a capacity that depends on having such-and-such disposition, it makes sense to conclude that *good* practical thought involves the proper exercise of that disposition. More generally, according to the con-structivist, good practical thought consists in the proper exercise of the dispositions in virtue of which one counts as a rational agent. The stan-dards of practical reason are thus derived from the nature of agency or practical thought.

This kind of constructivism can be found in a paper by Korsgaard that precedes *The Sources of Normativity*, one in which she imagines a capacity to respond to "pure practical reason" as something that "belongs to the subjective motivational set of every rational being" (1986: 328). For Korsgaard, this is the framework for a Kantian vindica-tion of moral reasons. If it is part of being a rational agent that one is disposed to give weight to considerations of humanity as an end in it-self—the argument runs—good practical thought depends in turn on the exercise of that disposition, so that considerations of humanity are reasons that apply to everyone. (To be a *rational* agent, in this context, is just to have the capacity for practical thought; it is not to meet some further evaluative standard.)

We can generalize from here. The claim is that the standards of practical thought correspond to dispositions that make up the capacity to engage in it. It is left completely open by the structure of this view just what these dispositions are: the tendency to will one's maxim as a universal law; to satisfy one's desires; to reflect on one's motives. Different proposals about the content of rational agency amount to different versions of constructivism, which need not have anything to do with Kant. Nor do they depend on the claim that practical thought is *about* what there is reason to do, or that, in acting for reasons, we take ourselves to have good reasons to act. On the face of it, at least, this is constructivism without the guise of the good.

What it does involve is commitment to a particular kind of *internalism* about practical reason, a certain way of hearing the claim that reasons must be "capable of motivating us" (Korsgaard 1986: 317). Reasons are capable of motivating, for the constructivist, because they correspond to dispositions that a rational agent must have. We can explain this claim as follows. Begin with the conceptual connection worked out in the introduction to this book:

> *Reasons*: The fact that p is a reason for A to ϕ just in case A has a collection of psychological states, C, such that the disposition to be moved to ϕ by C-and-the-belief-that-p is a good disposition of practical thought, and C contains no false beliefs.

Now, if good practical thought is the exercise of dispositions that constitute the *capacity* for practical thought, as our constructivist claims, it follows that as a rational agent—one who has that capacity—I must be disposed to engage in it. If the consideration that p is a reason for me to ϕ, I must already have the disposition to be moved to ϕ by some collection of my psychological states together with the belief that p. It does not follow that I will in fact be moved: dispositions can fail to operate, and the internalist need not believe that we are always responsive to reasons; she need not deny the possibility of what Korsgaard calls "true irrationality" (1986: 318–21). But if reasons correspond to dispositions that operate for the most part, or in the absence of interference, it does follow that, if the fact that p is a reason for me to ϕ, I am *capable* of being moved to ϕ by the belief that p.

The kind of constructivism we are examining, then, is equivalent to a certain sort of internalism about practical reason; it is a version of the internalist claim that reasons must be capable of motivating. I do not believe, however, that this connection offers any support for the constructivist. What it reveals is rather that, despite widespread adherence, internalism is not an innocuous claim, a platitude about reasons that everyone must respect. It is an ambitious and contentious view about the foundations of practical reason. This fact is masked by formulations that appeal to "practical rationality," as when it is said that reasons must be able to motivate us "insofar as we are rational" (Korsgaard 1986: 320) or "under conditions of *rational consideration*" (Darwall 1983: 81), or that "reasons for someone to do something must be considerations that would sway him toward doing it if he entertained them rationally" (Velleman 1996: 170). These claims can be read in a way that makes them completely harmless: it *is* a platitude—one expressed by *Reasons*—that an agent will be moved by a reason so long as she engages in good practical thought. It does not follow from this platitude that reasons are always capable of motivating us, unless we add that it is always within our capacities to engage in good practical thought. That is a wildly optimistic claim. Why suppose that anyone so much as capable of practical thought is capable of doing it well?[34]

In effect, this is a question about the *action theory* implicit in internalism. For the internalist, rational agency depends on dispositions that correspond to principles of practical reason: she hopes to find "a connection between the structure of a system of reasons and the structure of human motivation" (Nagel 1970: 32). In *The Possibility of Altruism*, Thomas Nagel argues that this connection can be made. According to Nagel, we cannot distinguish motivation from causal deviance, in the theory of action, except by supposing that motivation corresponds to good

---

[34] In pressing this question, I follow McDowell (1995a). I have elsewhere tried to diagnose one source of the internalist's optimism, in the doctrine that bad practical thought is a matter of *practical irrationality* (Setiya 2004a). In my view, there is a narrow sense of "irrationality" on which it implies not only a defect, but a *fault*, a sense in which it is a kind of *culpability*: "to call a person's action irrational is to a ascribe a certain kind of blame to the person" (White 1990: 412). Like moral blame, this depends on the capacity to do otherwise. If bad practical thought is always irrational in *this* sense, it must be something we have the capacity to avoid: if we are capable of reasoning at all, we must be capable of doing it well. The problem with this internalist argument is that there is no reason to suppose that bad practical thought is always irrational in the narrow sense that involves culpability, since there is no reason to suppose that we are always to blame for our defects of practical reason. We should not be led from this use of "practical irrationality" to the truth of the internalist claim. (In order to avoid confusion, it is worth noting a change of terminology. In the article cited here, I used the word "internalism" not for the conclusion of this argument—that reasons must be capable of motivating—but for its premise, that bad practical thought is always a matter of practical irrationality. What I take from the article is a reason for thinking that this premise is false.)

practical thought.[35] This is what makes it "intelligible" for me to put a dime in what I take to be a vending machine when I want a drink, but "unintelligible"—mere causal deviance—when I am led to put the dime in my pencil sharpener (Nagel 1970: 33–4). In the former case, but not the latter, I am moved by a *good* disposition of practical thought. Since dispositions of this kind are required by the capacity for motivation, and thus by the capacity for practical thought, they must belong to rational agents, as such.[36] Hence the rationalist or constructivist form of internalism about practical reason.

Nagel's argument has to be qualified.[37] As it stands, it leaves no room at all for *bad* practical thought, as when we are moved—not merely caused to act—in ways that do not correspond to principles of practical reason. What about the possibility of "true irrationality"? In order to allow for this, while keeping the connection between motivation and practical reason, Nagel must hold that, even when it goes awry, our practical thought can be described in terms of the frustrated operation of good dispositions, which therefore belong to us as rational agents. This is one version of a claim discussed at the end of Part One: the claim that motivational explanation—in particular, explanation by *reasons*—is "rationalizing" in that it shows an agent as having engaged in something approaching good practical thought.[38]

[35] This is the upshot of the complex dialectic in Nagel (1970: 30–35). What I take to be the same argument appears in Korsgaard (1997: 220–2), framed, unnecessarily, in terms of the guise of the good.

[36] Nagel is in fact more circumspect. He "prefer[s] to avoid any pronouncement about the modal status of [his] claims"—for instance, that he is investigating the *necessary conditions* of rational agency—and says more modestly that "if we were not [. . .] constituted [in the ways he describes], we should be unrecognizably different" (Nagel 1970: 19). As far as I can see, however, his argument depends on claims of the more ambitious kind.

[37] As well as the qualification in the text, we should note a limit to what the argument can show. It follows, at most, that in order to be capable of a particular *species* of practical thought, one must have the disposition to get it right. It does not follow that each instance of practical thought depends on having the whole array of good dispositions, if there are more than one. Instead motivation and practical thought may come in several forms—instrumental, prudential, other-regarding—each of which depends on a corresponding capacity for good practical thought of that specific form. If this is right, the nature of practical thought explains its distinctive standards, so that the Difference Principle is met, in much the way that the nature of crime explains the difference between a good crime and a good act. As I emphasized in section 2, this explanation does not depend on finding the aim or end of crime, as such, but on the fact that distinctive standards are introduced by each of its several forms—theft, arson, fraud, and all the rest. That corresponds to the structure of practical reason, in Nagel's account.

[38] I say that it is one version of this claim, and not the only one, because it is possible to *reject* internalism about practical reason while *accepting* a normative conception of reasons-explanation. See, for instance, McDowell (1985; 1995a). As I explain in the next paragraph,

Something like this picture *follows* from internalism about practical reason, considered as a form of constructivism. If the capacity for practical thought depends on having dispositions that correspond to principles of practical reason, and practical thought is, trivially, the exercise of this capacity, we cannot understand something as an instance of practical thought except by relating it to those dispositions, and thus to the standards of *good* practical thought.

The problem for the internalist is that, as I argued in Part One, there is nothing in the nature of action to support this view—nothing to suggest that, when we act for reasons, our practical thought must be even *approximately* good. (In particular, Nagel is wrong to suppose that we cannot distinguish motivation from causal deviance except in normative terms.) The mistake was to go from a general claim to one about particular cases. In general, the dispositions that govern our practical thought must be at least moderately good; there is a limit to the defects that are compatible with the capacity to think. But it does not follow that, in every instance, practical thought must be "made intelligible by being revealed to be, or to approximate to being, as [it] rationally ought to be" (McDowell 1985: 328). And it does not follow that a rational agent must have the whole array of good dispositions, a defeasible tendency *always* to engage in good practical thought. As before, that claim should look like a form of unreasonable optimism.

Unlike the traditional forms of Kantian constructivism, internalism about practical reason does not depend on the claim that, when we act for reasons, we take our reasons to be good. We have seen, however, that it does depend on a normative conception of reasons-explanation, on which our motivation is explained by the perhaps imperfect exercise of good dispositions of practical thought. It was a consequence of the final arguments of Part One that there is no basis for a normative conception of this kind in the abstract idea of acting for a reason.

If there is any prospect for internalism, as a form of constructivism, it will have to draw on more specific claims about the *elements* of practical thought, elements that appear in the theory of action defended in Part One. Despite its complexity, however, this theory was characterized by a kind of minimalism: it places few constraints on rational agents. So long as they are capable of *intention* and *motivation*, they can act for reasons. The internalist must hope to find grounds for a construction of practical reason in one of these two ideas. Each of them corresponds to a form of rationalism that I address in the rest of this book: the appeal to desire as a condition of motivation, in section 4, and, in section 5, the idea that

---

the connection I am addressing runs the other way: *from* internalism *to* the idea that motivation depends on good dispositions of practical thought.

practical reason turns on the involvement of self-knowledge in the intention to act. I will argue that, just as there is no general ground for sympathy with the constructivist project, we ought to reject it even in its most promising and realistic forms.

4. Motivation and Desire

According to the *instrumentalist*, the object of practical reason is the satisfaction of desire. More carefully, our dispositions of practical thought are good, as such, just to the extent that we are *means-end efficient*. In this context, "efficiency" is a term of art: to be efficient is to be disposed to want, and to take, the apparent means to the satisfaction of one's final desires. This disposition is distinct from, and broader than, the tendency to conform to Kant's hypothetical imperative. His requirement is to will what one thinks of as the *necessary* means to ends that one *intends* to bring about. It does not apply to less-than-necessary means, or to desires on which one does not yet intend to act. It is therefore silent about the balancing of desires and probabilities in practical thought, and about the best way to achieve a plurality of potentially conflicting ends. (The hypothetical imperative is not fit to serve as a general theory of practical reason.) By contrast, it is part of being efficient, in the instrumentalist's sense, that one be disposed to choose in ways that will satisfy one's final desires, taken together and balanced against one another, in the light of one's beliefs. A proper theory of efficiency would have to incorporate a story about this, an account of the proper trade-offs among desires one cannot be sure of satisfying all at once.[39]

This is not the only respect in which the instrumentalist's conception of practical reason as efficiency is richer than we might suppose. For instance, we should allow for an extended or inclusive concept of *means*, one that covers both *productive* and *constitutive* means to an end. A productive means is an efficient cause; a constitutive means is one that is an instance of, or part of, the relevant end. Thus moving the brush against the canvas is a constitutive means to painting, in that it is an *instance* of painting; putting on my socks is a constitutive means to getting dressed, in that it is *part* of getting dressed. With a theory of balancing, and the broader notion of a means, the instrumentalist can accommodate at least some cases of deliberation by imaginative "specification," as when I try

---

[39] It is in the context of this demand that the technical apparatus of decision theory may have some appeal—see, especially, Hampton (1998, ch. 7)—though its success in this role is controversial. On the distinction between the hypothetical imperative and the idea of balancing among desires in general, see Korsgaard (1997: 215–7 and 1999 *passim*.)

to figure out not what would *cause* but what would *be* a fun holiday, or a satisfying profession.[40]

In each of these cases, efficiency can be thought of as the disposition that governs the transition to new intentions and desires—ones that aim at the best causal or constitutive means to getting what one finally wants. Efficiency is thus a kind of motivating state: not just a matter of knowing the means to one's ends, but of being motivated to take them. This is consistent with the common instrumentalist refrain that reason is "motivationally inert," since the role of efficiency is merely to transmit motivation from one's final desires to further intentions or desires; it is not an *original* source of motivation.

The topic of this section is not instrumentalism in general—I return to that, briefly, in the conclusion of the book—but instrumentalism in its rationalist or constructivist form. The ethical rationalist purports to derive the standards of practical reason, at least in outline, from the nature of practical thought. In doing so, she hopes to meet the challenge posed by the Difference Principle. If dispositions of practical thought are subject to distinctive standards, apart from those of good character, there must be something about the nature of practical thought, or the dispositions that govern it, to explain or illuminate the difference. For the instrumentalist who is also an ethical rationalist, the object of practical reason is the satisfaction of our final desires *because* these desires have a special role to play in practical thought.

The simplest proposal of this kind would hold that practical thought takes place "under the guise of desire," in that it aims *explicitly* at the satisfaction of desire. For instance, the claim would go, in acting for a reason one must take oneself to have a final desire whose object one's action would, or might conceivably, help to achieve. Hence the standard of good practical thought is that it promotes the general satisfaction of one's desires, in light of one's beliefs. This is not a plausible line for the instrumentalist to take. We can engage in practical thought, and act for reasons, without relying on beliefs about our own desires, as such. In the language of Pettit and Smith, such desires need not appear in the *foreground* of practical thought, even if their presence is somehow required (1990). Practical thought may be driven by desire, but that is not what it is *about*. What the instrumentalist needs—assuming that she aspires to rationalism—is a picture on which our final desires figure essentially in the *background* of practical thought, directing its progress without having to appear in it, as objects.

---

[40] On deliberation by specification, see Wiggins (1975/6: 225 and *passim*), Kolnai (1977), and Richardson (1994).

The most promising suggestion, here, is that dispositions of practical thought, through which we form and revise our intentions and desires, must be triggered partly by desire. This has to be qualified: even the instrumentalist will concede that a mere change of belief can affect desire, as when I realize that an action is *not*, after all, a means to my end, and thus give up my intention to do it. The claim must be restricted to dispositions of practical thought through which we form *new* intentions and desires: desire can figure in the output of a disposition only if it figures as an input, too. It follows that the dispositions of practical thought through which we form intentions to act must be triggered ultimately by desires that are not derived from practical thought, and thus by final desires.[41] If dispositions of practical thought are in this way fueled by desire, that would explain why they are subject to a standard of their own—not just the standard of good character, but one that has to do with the satisfaction of desire. This is enough to meet the modest demand set by the Difference Principle. It would explain why means-end efficiency, not ethical virtue, is the standard for good dispositions of practical thought.

The doctrine I have attributed to the instrumentalist, as the premise for a form of ethical rationalism, is related to what is nowadays called the "Humean theory of motivation."[42] According to the Humean theory, intentional action must be explained in part by a prior desire, as must desires that arise from practical thought—what Nagel calls "motivated desires" (1970: 29–30). This follows from the instrumentalist's premise, that dispositions of practical thought must be triggered partly by desire. (The Humean has a further commitment, that desires are to be conceived as thoroughly *non-cognitive* states: there are no "besires," no beliefs that have desiderative force, or that entail the presence of desire.[43] This claim is not involved in the instrumentalist's construction of practical reason. We can count as a "desire" whatever entails that there is something an agent *wants*, in the least restrictive sense of "want.")

In order to satisfy the Difference Principle, then, the instrumentalist needs the part of the Humean theory that requires the motivation of action and desire always to be traced in part to a prior desire, where it is

---

[41] This argument assumes that a desire is final if it does not derive from practical thought. It does not depend on the converse claim, that a desire cannot be final if it does derive from practical thought. It has been argued—albeit controversially—that even the instrumentalist can make sense of the reasoned revision of final desires. See Harman (1976: 174), Frankfurt (1992) and Schmidtz (1994).

[42] See, especially, Smith (1987). As I argue in section 2 of Setiya (2004c), Hume did not accept the "Humean theory." But the label has stuck, and I will drop the scare quotes from now on.

[43] For the language of "besire," see Altham (1986).

not assumed that desires are categorically distinct from beliefs. This fact, I think, explains the persistent sense that there is a path from the Humean theory of motivation to instrumentalism about practical reason. The most influential argument here is due to Bernard Williams (1980: 106–9). Setting aside some complications, his point is that we can go from *internalism* about practical reason, together with the Humean theory, to the truth of instrumentalism.[44] If reasons must be able to motivate us, and motivation always depends on final desires, our reasons must depend in turn on the content of our final desires. This argument has been criticized in various ways; the details are controversial. But the real problem is that it depends on a kind of internalism we are not entitled to take for granted. (This is the moral of the arguments at the end of section 3.) The rationalist argument is both more modest, and more effective: it does not presuppose internalism about practical reason in deriving its standards from the nature of practical thought.

Nevertheless, I think the rationalist form of instrumentalism is false. There is no reason to believe that dispositions of practical thought that generate new intentions or desires must be triggered in part by previous ones. The standard argument for the Humean theory is defective. And while there may be a sense in which desire is always involved in practical thought, this sense is not enough to support the premise that the rationalist needs. It is not enough to show that dispositions of practical thought must always be triggered partly by desire. In the rest of this section, I explain and defend these claims.

The seminal discussion of the Humean theory of motivation is due to Michael Smith (1987). Arguments for the Humean theory were almost non-existent before his paper appeared, and they have since consisted in variations on his theme. Part of his argument is concerned with "direction of fit" and the rejection of "besires." This has already been discussed, in another context; and it is in any case irrelevant here.[45] We are interested in the argument that motivation always depends on a prior desire. Smith's treatment of this point is embedded in a terminology I want to do without: the language of "motivating reasons" criticized and rejected in Part One, most explicitly at the beginning of section 2. This will require some reconstructive work, through which, I think, the spirit of his argument survives.

We begin with Smith's principal formulation:

(1) Having a motivating reason *is, inter alia,* having a goal.

[44] For further discussion of this putative connection, see Nagel (1970: 27–9), Bond (1983: 6–7), Korsgaard (1986: 220–6), and Wallace (1990: 356ff.), among others.
[45] The discussion appears near the beginning of Part One, section 4. It is irrelevant here because the instrumentalist need not deny the possibility of "besires."

(2) Having a goal *is* being in a state with which the world must fit.

and

(3) Being in a state with which the world must fit *is* desiring. (Smith 1987: 55)

The conclusion of this argument is that having a motivating reason *is*, *inter alia*, having a desire. Before I attempt to paraphrase Smith's use of "motivating reasons," I want to simplify his argument in another way. We can ignore the technical concept of a "state with which the world must fit," and simply assume that having a goal is an instance of "desire," in the modest sense with which we are concerned. If someone has a goal, they must be in a state we can report by saying that there is something they want. This fact can play the role of premise (2) and premise (3). Everything depends on premise (1): the alleged connection between having a motivating reason and having a goal. Since a motivating reason is a state that is "*potentially explanatory* of [action]" (Smith 1987: 38), the first premise of Smith's argument is that a state that can motivate action must constitute one's having a goal. The difficulty is to be clear about "potential explanation" and the motivation of action. The Humean claim is not just that desire must figure *somewhere* in the explanation of action, but that intentional action is always "at bottom" motivated by desire. Its explanation can be traced, in the end, to desires that are not derived from practical thought. Smith needs to establish *both* that a state that can motivate action constitutes one's having a goal *and* that the same is true of a state that can motivate intention or desire. Without the second claim, we leave room for the motivation of action by a desire that is motivated, in turn, by belief alone: we leave room for intentional action that is, at bottom, motivated solely by belief.[46]

Of the two claims that Smith must establish, the first is pretty obviously true. It is in any case vindicated by the arguments of Part One. Intentional action is always explained, in part, by the desire-like belief that constitutes one's *intention* in acting, and thus by a desire. The problem is with the second claim. For, while it is plausible to regard intentional action as essentially the execution of an intention, it is very odd to say the same thing

---

[46] It is not clear to me that Smith fully appreciates this point, which is due to Nagel (1970: 29–30). He seems to argue for both claims in "The Humean Theory of Motivation" (1987); but the argument for the second, discussed below, is dropped from the presentation of the Humean theory in his later book (1994, ch. 4), and he apparently allows for desires that are motivated by beliefs, and dispositions or tendencies that are not desires, alone. The last point is especially clear in Smith (1998: 167–9). It is possible that Smith's version of the Humean theory does not include the second claim distinguished in the text—in which case it cannot help the instrumentalist who hopes for a form of ethical rationalism.

about the motivation of intention or desire. Typically, when a desire is formed in practical thought, one does not *intend* to form that desire; one does not form it as a means or as an end; one does not think about the desire, as such. It follows that we cannot iterate the argument about the motivation of action, as an argument about the motivation of desire. But that is precisely what Smith attempts to do. He argues that "[a] motivated desire is a desire had for a reason; that is, a desire the having of which furthers some goal that the agent has" (Smith 1987: 59), and thus a desire that is motivated *by* desire. This makes it sound as though I am moved to perform the action of acquiring the desire, on the ground that having it will serve a useful purpose. Even if this is possible, it is not the usual case.[47] In forming a desire in practical thought, one is normally concerned with the *object* of that desire, not with the desire itself; one does not have the *goal* of forming the desire, or a goal that one expects to be advanced by having it. It follows that we cannot model the motivation of desire on the motivation of action. The considerations that support the modest claim, that intentional action is always motivated by desire, cannot be made to support the Humean theory in general.

If this is right, Smith's argument fails because it harbours a conflation that is partly masked by the idea of a motivating reason. The question is whether it can be repaired—whether there are considerations in the vicinity of his account that might support a Humean claim about the motivation of desire. The most persuasive line appeals to the suggestion that desire can be conceived in *dispositional* terms.[48] In brief, the argument is this:

> Suppose for *reductio* that I form a new desire on the basis of psychological states that do not include a prior desire. In order to have a specific example, we can imagine that I form the desire to help you move your furniture because I come to believe that you need help—even though I have no general desire to help you, or to help anyone in need. I am simply moved, on this occasion, by the fact that you can't manage on your own. Surely we must concede, the Humean insists, that I was *disposed* to form the new desire on the basis of that belief. But on a suitably relaxed conception, this disposition *itself* should count as a desire. It is a state whose presence entails that there is something I want, namely: to help you move your furniture if you need help. So my new desire was formed, after all, on the basis of a prior desire, a desire whose content is a conditional.

[47] Its possibility is a question raised by Kavka's "toxin puzzle" (1983).

[48] This is proposed by Smith (1987, section 5), drawing on a broadly functionalist conception of the mind. Compare Stalnaker: "To desire that P is to be disposed to act in ways that would bring it about that P in a world in which one's beliefs, whatever they are, were true" (1984: 15).

I think this argument is the best that can be done for the Humean theory of motivation. It makes a number of controversial claims: first, in attributing a disposition to support the explanatory connection between belief and desire; second, in proposing that this disposition amounts to a desire for the truth of a conditional claim.[49] It also faces a substantial and perhaps decisive objection, that it cannot work in general. How could it apply, for instance, to the motivation of desire not by belief, but by other cognitive states? Suppose that I form the desire to abolish capital punishment only when I come to imagine conditions on death row—conditions that I believed to obtain all along. While the disposition to form a desire on the basis of a belief may be thought of as desiring a conditional, what is the content of my disposition to be moved by an imaginative state? It does not seem to entail that there is anything I *want*; it is just a disposition.[50]

I propose to set these issues aside. Even if we grant that desires that arise in practical thought must be explained by states that count as prior desires, that is not enough to establish the claim that the instrumentalist needs. The premise of the rationalist argument was that dispositions of practical thought that generate new desires must be triggered in part by the presence of prior desires. That is why such dispositions are subject to a distinctive standard, of means-end efficiency. This premise is stronger than the conclusion of the argument above, that new desires must always derive from old ones. We can see the distinction in our example. It is one thing to say that my disposition is itself a desire, so that my desire to help you with your furniture is explained in part by a prior desire. It is another thing to say that my disposition is *not* a disposition of practical thought, since if it were, there would be at least one such disposition that is triggered by belief alone. The rationalist must defend the second claim, that my disposition-or-desire is not a disposition of practical thought in its own right. It must be conceived, instead, as the input to a *further* disposition, the *real* disposition of practical thought, which is, therefore, triggered partly by desire. But there is no need for a further disposition here. It is sufficient to explain my practical thought in wanting to help you move your furniture that I had the disposition to be moved by the belief

[49] As I read them, Pettit and Price (1989: 165–6) would reject both of these claims; Parfit would reject the second (1997: 105). But the first claim seems plausible to me, on the assumption that my belief does not itself entail the presence of desire (cf. Pettit and Price 1989: 168–9). And the second claim may be defensible too. The idea that desiring a conditional is being disposed to form an unconditional desire on the basis of a belief is modeled on Mellor's theory of *believing* a conditional, as the disposition to infer one belief from another (1993).

[50] As Dreier says, "desires are typed by their content"; in specifying them, "[we] can't just cite inputs and outputs" (1997: 94).

that you need help. To require a further disposition is to embark on a vicious regress.

We can put the point in more positive terms. It is clear that my desire to help you out is a product of practical thought, in the unambitious sense I have employed throughout this book. So it had better be explained by a disposition of practical thought. But the only disposition required is the disposition to form a new desire because I believe that you need help. It follows that this disposition, even if it counts as a desire, must be a disposition of practical thought. Hence, a disposition of practical thought that generates a new desire need *not* be triggered, even in part, by a prior desire. The premise of the rationalist argument is false.

This conclusion marks the failure of instrumentalism, at least in its rationalist form.[51] If dispositions of practical thought can be triggered by belief alone, there is no reason to suppose that they are subject to a distinctive standard of means-end efficiency. How could that standard so much as be applied to dispositions like mine?

The argument of this section supports a more general moral. I have been examining the prospects for ethical rationalism, as the only possible response to the argument of section 2. That argument posed a dilemma: we have to choose between rationalism and the virtue theory of practical reason. In this section, I have argued that the rationalist cannot appeal to the role of desire in practical thought so as to justify a form of instrumentalism. I think we can make a stronger claim. Once we reject the guise of the good, and the idea that dispositions of practical thought must be triggered partly by desire, we are left with very minimal constraints on the *motivation* of intention and desire. There is nothing in these constraints that could supply the needs of the ethical rationalist. The consequence is that she has only one place left to look: if rationalism is true, the standards of practical reason must derive, at least in outline, from the nature of *intention*, and its role in causing us to act. What is distinctive of intention, on my account, is that it involves beliefs about the explanation of action. The thought must be that this feature of intention is what satisfies the Difference Principle. It is because dispositions of practical thought motivate action through intention,

---

[51] Dreier defends a somewhat different form of instrumentalist rationalism, according to which the disposition to be efficient, at least to some extent, is an essential condition of rational agency (1997: 96), so that a global failure of efficiency is simply impossible (1997: 98). Efficiency is in this way *special*. If I am right to argue that dispositions of practical thought can be triggered by belief alone, however, Dreier's first claim is false: one can engage in practical thought without having to rely on prior desires. What *is* true is that an agent with final desires cannot be *generally* disposed to want what she knows to be bad means to her ends. But this is simply a consequence of the constitutive ideal of rationality, the fact that our practical thought cannot be all bad. It is not a special fact about practical thought that is driven by desire.

which is reflexive desire-like belief, that they are subject to a standard of their own—not just the standard of good character, but one that has to do with *self-knowledge*. This idea has been advanced by David Velleman, in *Practical Reflection* and *The Possibility of Practical Reason*.[52] In the following section, I argue that, although there is a sense in which self-knowledge is the aim of intentional action, it cannot provide the foundation for a theory of reasons to act.

5. SELF-KNOWLEDGE AS THE AIM OF ACTION

The argument of this section has three parts. In the first, I explain why I agree with Velleman that the constitutive aim of action is self-knowledge. In the second, I argue against Velleman's conception of this aim as a general tendency, one that interacts an agent's beliefs about himself. And in the final part, I turn to the philosophy of practical reason. In order to derive the standards of practical reason from self-knowledge as the aim of action, we would have to rely on Velleman's dubious conception of this constitutive aim—a conception that I reject.

My agreement with Velleman begins with the claim that intentional action is *self-explanatory*. We can derive this curious fact from the argument of Part One, as follows. When someone acts intentionally, she must be doing something she intends to do; and the content of her intention is a motivational explanation of what she is doing. If nothing else, the intention represents *itself* as motivating her to act. ("I am hereby doing ϕ.") But when we act for reasons—because p, or for the sake of doing ϕ—it is more expansive. The desire-like belief that constitutes one's intention, in such a case, contains an explanation of action partly in terms of the belief that p, or the desire to ϕ (and the belief that one's action is a means to doing ϕ), and what one intends is to be acting-because-p or for-the-sake-of-doing-ϕ.

If all goes well, one's intentional action makes the content of one's intention true. At the very least, one must be performing the *action* one intends—one must be doing ϕ in order to be doing ϕ intentionally. And except in the very peculiar case of self-deceptive action—where the explanatory part of one's intention is false—one is motivated in the way that one intends to be.[53] Because intention involves *belief*, it follows that intentional action is a source of self-knowledge, a source of true beliefs about one's action and its psychological explanation.

---

[52] Velleman (1989; 2000b).
[53] Self-deceptive action was examined, briefly, in Part One, section 3.

But intention is not simply belief; it is *desire-like* belief. It tends to motivate the action it depicts, and to make it be caused or motivated in the way that it depicts. So, when "all goes well" and one does act as one intends, one comes to have true beliefs about one's action and its explanation for which one's intention is itself responsible. It is a general fact about intentional action that, since it is motivated by intention, it is motivated in such a way as to provide us with knowledge about ourselves. This tendency belongs to the nature of intentional action, as such. And it provides a modest sense in which self-knowledge can be described as the constitutive aim of action: it is a goal towards which intentional action is always and essentially directed.[54]

It is easy to scoff at this suggestion, but not, I think, when it is properly understood. The first step is to stress—as Velleman (2000b: 19–21) does—that the constitutive aim of action is not a matter of *desire*.[55] In *The Possibility of Practical Reason*, he argues that "self-knowledge is the constitutive aim of action" (2000b: 26), even though it is not an aim that *agents* necessarily have, or something that figures in the foreground of their practical thought (see Velleman 2000b: 19–21). That fits with the present account: my claim is not that, as agents, we *want* to understand ourselves, or that, in acting intentionally, we *intend* to gain self-knowledge, as such, but that, necessarily, intentional action is directed towards that goal, since the execution of one's intention *is*, at the same time, the achievement of knowledge about what one is doing and why.

Despite agreeing with Velleman that intentional action aims at self-knowledge, and that its having this aim is not a matter of the agent's intention or desire, I want to contrast his robust conception of the constitutive aim of action with the modest one that I defend. (This difference will be crucial to questions of practical reason.) For Velleman, the constitutive aim of action is a *tendency* that operates in the agent, one that drives him towards self-knowledge: it motivates him to act in ways that he will understand, and prevents him from acting in ways that he will not. This tendency is something we "add to subjects of motivation [who are not yet capable of *intentional* action] in order to create agents" (2000b: 26). It is a tendency that interacts with an agent's beliefs about what he is doing, or what he is going to do, and why. (It is important to

---

[54] A more cautious statement of the point would hedge the distinction between knowledge and true belief. There are difficult questions about the epistemology of practical knowledge, which we set aside in the first section of Part One.

[55] Here he is withdrawing some of what he says in *Practical Reflection*, where he claims that, as a rational agent, you have a "desire not just to know but also to understand what you're doing" (Velleman 1989: 27).

stress that it interacts with such beliefs, in general, not with some special subset of beliefs, or with intentions as desire-like beliefs.) For Velleman, an *agent* is by nature disposed to act in ways that he will understand, and not disposed to act in ways that he will not. When this tendency operates in the motivation of action, causing one to act in a way one understands, it constitutes that action *as* intentional. And by *preventing* us from acting in ways that we will not understand, the tendency "explain[s] why, in the normal case, you already know what you're doing, or at least trying to do, without ever finding out" (Velleman 1989: 26).

I do not believe that the tendency Velleman describes is one that belongs to rational agents, as such: its exercise is not required in acting for reasons. If the account in Part One is right, there is no need to appeal to this tendency in the explanation of intentional action. According to that account, intention is desire-like belief, and if all goes well, intentional action provides self-knowledge by making the content of one's intention true. It does not follow from this that, as rational agents, we are generally disposed to act in ways that confirm our beliefs about ourselves. It is our *intentions* that motivate us, in particular, not mere beliefs about what we are doing, or what we are going to do, and why.

The central difference between Velleman's account and mine is that I take intention to be a distinctive sort of psychological state, one that has some features of belief—for instance, it may count as knowledge—together with the motivating force that we associate with desire. Velleman's tendency is part of a reductive theory of intention, in this sense. He means to account for the phenomenon of desire-like belief in terms of the interaction of general tendency towards self-knowledge with ordinary beliefs about oneself.[56] But there is no motivation for reduction here, at least if I was right to argue (at the beginning of Part One, section 4) that we can make good sense of desire-like belief, in its own right. There is no reason not to take the appearance at face value. It is one's *intentions* that motivate action, not mere beliefs about oneself.

There is, in any case, a powerful argument against the tendency account. It generates what Michael Bratman calls the "problem of promiscuity" (1991: 261–2). If Velleman is right, we should expect to be moved to act in ways that confirm our beliefs about ourselves, in general—and this does not seem to be the case. I may believe that I am about to trip over a doorstep, or that I am the sort of person who is bad at keeping secrets, so that a tendency towards self-knowledge would be satisfied by tripping, or breaking a confidence, without being *motivated* to do these things, in light of my belief. Velleman seems wrong to say that these are

---

[56] See Velleman (1989, chs. 3–4; 1996: 194–6; 2000b: 22–26).

merely cases in which the relevant motivation is swamped or over-whelmed (1989: 54–5); on the face of it, there is no motivation here at all. On this point, the present theory of action and intention disagrees with Velleman, and agrees with common sense.[57]

But the main point is not empirical; it is about the *possibility* of rational agents that do not have a general tendency towards self-knowledge. This possibility is established by Part One. So long as one has desire-like beliefs to play the role of intending and taking as one's reason, one's practical thought need not involve the tendency that Velleman describes. One need not be moved by any old belief about what one is doing, or what one is going to do—only by one's *intentions*. Velleman's tendency does not be-long to the *essence* of rational agency; and so it is not among the materials to which the rationalist can appeal.

The question, then, is whether a more deflationary conception of the aim of action as self-knowledge will be enough to satisfy the Difference Principle: to derive the standards of practical reason, in outline, from the nature of practical thought. Predictably, I want to argue that it will not. This comes out most vividly if we work with Velleman's schema for the construction of practical reason. His claim is that "the constitutive aim of action determines an internal criterion of success for action, in relation to which considerations qualify as reasons for acting" (Velleman 2000b: 26). In particular, if the constitutive aim of action is motivational self-knowledge, reasons to act are precisely "considerations that would pro-vide the subject with an explanatory grasp of the behavior for which they are reasons" (2000b: 26). Velleman's account thus moves directly from the aim of action to reasons for doing things, without taking an intermedi-ate step through (good) dispositions of practical thought. (This economy is harmless if, as I argued in the introduction, claims about reasons are conceptually equivalent to claims of the latter kind.)

---

[57] More recently, Velleman has argued that empirical work in "self psychology" supports the attribution of a tendency to act in way that verify our self-conceptions (2000c). This deserves a full discussion, which I cannot hope to undertake here. Here are three points, in brief. First, it is clear that the evidence that Velleman cites is somewhat equivocal, and that his preferred interpretation is controversial, as he is willing to concede. We can account for much of the evidence in more prosaic terms—for example, when I come to see myself as generous, I will try to live up to that flattering description; when I come to see myself as an inveterate liar, I won't bother to struggle against my inclination to lie. Neither explanation depends on a tendency towards self-knowledge. Second, I cannot see anything in the litera-ture that Velleman cites that would apply to such mundane examples as tripping over the doorstep. Third, it is of course consistent with my account that most of us *do* want to think of ourselves in simple and unified ways. The question is whether this common desire is presupposed by the very capacity to act for reasons. In the previous paragraph—and, in effect, in the whole of Part One—I have argued that it is not.

How could Velleman's proposal be applied? The basic idea would be that, if someone is acting in a way that makes true the explanatory content of her intention, her action satisfies its constitutive aim (by providing her with knowledge of herself) and therefore satisfies the standards of practical reason, at least to some extent. Provided that she is acting as she intends, and that she is motivated in the way that her intention describes, her action is not only explained by reasons, but *justified*. A problem is immediately apparent here. If acting in accordance with one's intention is sufficient to satisfy the constitutive aim of action, and thereby sufficient for doing what there is most reason to do, the standards of practical reason are too easy to meet. One falls short of these standards only when there is a mis-match between the content of one's intention, including its explanatory content, and what one actually does. So, for instance, I may not be adjusting the brightness of my television screen, even though I intend to be, because I am wrong about which button does what. Or I may be mistaken about my motives: I mean to be working because I enjoy it, but what really drives me is the fear of failure. So long as I do not go wrong in either of these ways, however, my action makes the explanatory content of my intention true, and thus provides me with knowledge of myself. If this is enough to satisfy the standards of practical reason, they are satisfied whenever we act in the way that we intend to act. But that cannot be right: the standards of practical reason must be ones that we can violate, even when we know what we are doing and why. They are, among other things, standards for the *evaluation* of what we do, in this effective and undeceived way.

Velleman's solution to this problem is to argue that the constitutive aim of action can be satisfied by *degree*, so that one counts as acting on the best reasons only if one's achievement of this aim is perfect or ideal. This was implicit in my initial application of his idea, where I said that, in making true the content of one's intention, one meets the standards of practical reason *to some extent*. It does not follow, so the argument goes, that one has managed to act as one should, all things considered. As I see it, this refinement is a central part of Velleman's view. He discusses an example in which I make true my prediction that I am going to shout out of anger precisely by shouting, but in which we do not want to say that my action was fully justified (see Velleman 1989: 54–5). His response is that, while my anger provides *some* justification for my action, this justification is overwhelmed, because I could achieve much *greater* self-knowledge by holding my tongue. Assuming that I have strong motives for keeping quiet, ones with which I am closely identified, the explanation of action that I would make true by doing so, on the basis of those motives, would be more edifying than the explanation I make true by shouting. It would constitute a deeper, more subtle, and more satisfying contribution to my self-understanding. In keeping quiet, I would satisfy the aim of self-knowledge as well as I possibly could, in this circumstance. So even though there is a reason for me to shout, there is more reason for me to hold my tongue.[58] This appeal to degrees of self-knowledge—to the idea that it can be more or less edifying, and thus achieve the constitutive aim of action more or less well—seems to me the pivotal move in Velleman's theory of practical reason. It is the move that promises to solve the problem raised in the previous paragraph, and so to take us from the aim of action to defensible conclusions about what there is reason to do.[59]

Despite its ingenuity, however, this solution does not work: it mis-conceives the *way* in which intentional action aims at self-knowledge. On the theory of Part One, the truth behind the metaphor of a constitutive aim is that one's intention in acting is a desire-like belief about the motivation of one's action, which its execution would make true. This aim is in no way *better* achieved if the explanation that figures in the intention is of one sort or another: an elaborate description of one's deepest character rather than a superficial appeal to whim. Insofar as acting on one's intention is a matter of making true its explanatory content, and thus gaining self-knowledge, it achieves this aim equally and perfectly well regardless of the nature of the explanation. Success in action, in the sense defined by its constitutive aim, *is* simply a matter of doing what one intends. The pivotal move in Velleman's theory—that of construing the aim of action as something that is satisfied to a greater or lesser degree, in proportion to the depth of self-knowledge one gains—turns essentially on the bad conception of the aim of action as, if not a desire, then at least a tendency towards greater and more profound self-understanding. It *would* make sense to think of a tendency towards self-knowledge as something that is better satisfied by "deeper" or "greater" self-knowledge. But, as I argued at the beginning of this section, that tendency is not required for the motivation of intentional action.

At this point, the proponent of Velleman's approach may offer the following argument:

---

[58] The same story is told, in relation to a different example, at Velleman (2000b: 29); see also Velleman (1989: 39–40, 204–5).

[59] It is worth asking whether the consequences of this theory are in fact sufficiently plausible. They continue to be, in a certain way, *permissive*. If the fundamental prescription of practical reason is "to thine own self be true," then Claudius may well have done that he *should* have done in killing Hamlet's father. After all, despite his guilt, he cannot repent; this is who he is. If one is vicious through and through, on the present account, it seems that one *ought* to act in vicious ways. Velleman spends the last few chapters of *Practical Reflection* arguing that such implications are merely apparent; his view agrees with common sense about moral and prudential reasons. These arguments seem doubtful to me—but I do not have space to press my worries here.

(1) Even on the modest construal of its constitutive aim, intentional action is, among other things, action that gives one knowledge of oneself; it is the source of an explanatory theory of one's own psychology.

(2) But, as a quite general matter, a theory is better, as such, if it is deeper and more explanatory; insofar as one is engaged in the project of explanation, one does a good job just to the extent that one's theory is *edifying*.

(3) It follows that, as an attempt to gain self-knowledge, intentional action is better, as such, if the self-knowledge it provides is deeper and more explanatory; one acts well just to the extent that one acts so as to a make true an edifying theory of oneself.

This tempting line is mistaken in two ways. First, on the necessary interpretation, premise (2) is false. Distinguish two claims: (i) that *active inquiry* is good, as such, only to the extent that it delivers deep and explanatory theories; and (ii) that an agent's *beliefs* are epistemically good only to the extent that they form part of an edifying explanatory system. The first claim may be true; but it is irrelevant, since intentional action does not *explicitly* aim at self-knowledge. In acting intentionally, one is not directing an inquiry into oneself; self-knowledge is not one's *end*. The second claim *might* engage with our picture of intentional action, since it speaks about the epistemic quality of the desire-like belief that constitutes intention. But the claim is false: there is nothing epistemically defective, or imperfect, in true beliefs whose contents are not edifying at all. Even those who think that belief revision is *always* a matter of increasing explanatory coherence admit that epistemic norms do not require us to reflect on everything, to make *all* of our beliefs into unified theories. There is nothing wrong with my (true) beliefs about American history, just on the ground that the story they tell is superficial and full of holes. I am simply not interested. The obligation to develop unified theories is an obligation to develop such theories about the things one has picked out as objects of inquiry. In picking out such objects, one need not pick oneself.

The second problem with the argument is in the step from (1) and (2) to (3). Even if we grant the problematic reading of premise (2), on which beliefs are better in epistemic terms to the extent that they form an edifying theory, it does not follow that intentional action is better, as such, if the self-knowledge it provides is deeper and more explanatory. Once again, we have to bear in mind the attributive character of *good*. In this context, the crucial point is to distinguish being good in *epistemic* terms or *qua belief*, from being good in *practical* terms. Suppose it is true that my intention is epistemically defective, because it presents me as being motivated by a momentary flash of emotion, not by my long-standing goals and commitments. How is it supposed to follow that, when I am acting on this intention, my *action* is defective, that there is something wrong with *it*? After all, so far as the practical-motivational side is concerned, my intention is doing its job: it is motivating me to act in a way that makes it true. An argument is required to eliminate the standard distinction between epistemic and practical evaluation—and we have no hint as to what this argument could be.

Things might look different if Velleman were right about the *way* in which intentional action aims at self-knowledge. For, on his account, the tendency by which such action is produced is a tendency towards self-knowledge, and thus, we naturally suppose, a tendency that is satisfied in proportion to the degree or depth of self-knowledge we achieve. Here the demand for edification is built into the content of the tendency that forms the aim of action; it is not something we try to recover just from the role of belief in intending to act. By contrast, if we restrict ourselves to the modest sense in which intentional action aims at self-knowledge, the sense for which I have argued above, we find that there is no way to support the pivotal move in Velleman's argument—the appeal to *degrees* of self-knowledge—by which we might hope to derive a substantive theory of reasons to act.

My conclusion, then, is that in the only sense in which intentional action may truly be said to have a constitutive aim, the achievement of this aim is not enough to satisfy the standards of practical reason. More generally, there is no way to derive those standards, not even in outline, from the nature of agency or practical thought. My argument supports this categorical claim, despite its structure—examining a series of proposals in turn—because the Part One theory of intentional action gives no purchase to the project of ethical rationalism. It gives sufficient conditions of acting for a reason that leave the form and content of practical thought insufficiently constrained for them to set its distinctive standards.

In acting for a reason, one is moved to form a reflexive desire-like belief (intention) about one's action, which is then responsible for moving one to act. It follows that the rationalist must appeal to the nature of *intention* or *motivation* in deriving the standards of practical thought. That is why the critical arguments above can claim to be exhaustive: they consider both possibilities, and these are the only possibilities there are. The moral of section 5 is that the standards of practical reason cannot derive from the nature of intention, as desire-like belief about oneself: Velleman's project does not work. And the moral of sections 3 and 4 is that they cannot derive from the nature of *motivation*. The constitutive ideal of rationality is the only real constraint on our motivational dispositions: taken together with our beliefs and desires, they must be at least moderately sane. (See the end of Part One.) This tells us nothing about the *content* of practical reason. Nor should we accept the more ambitious doctrines—about the guise of the good, or the dependence of practical thought upon desire—which might be thought to play that role. If this is right, Part One ensures that there is nowhere else to look: there is nothing in the nature of agency or practical thought, as a matter of intention and motivation, from which the standards of practical reason could derive.

It follows in turn that there is no way to satisfy the Difference Principle—no way to explain how the standards of practical reason come apart from those of ethical virtue. The idea that dispositions of practical thought are subject to different modes of assessment—as dispositions to reason well, and as good traits of character—is an illusion fostered by ethical rationalism. When that illusion is dissolved, I have argued, the consequence is not scepticism, but the virtue theory of practical reason. Aristotle was right: we cannot be fully good without the perfection of practical reason, or have that perfection without being good.

THE ARGUMENT of this book begins with the fact that dispositions of practical thought belong to one's character. Its crucial premise—which depends on rejecting the guise of the good—is that they are not distinguished from other traits of character in a way that would explain why they are subject to their own evaluative standard; ethical rationalism is false. Its conclusion—which follows by the Difference Principle—is that the property of being good as a disposition of practical thought is the property (of such dispositions) of being good as a trait of character. That is why the virtue theory of practical reason is true.

The consequence is that we have to bring our convictions about what there is reason to do into harmony with our convictions about the virtues of character. These concepts are connected by a pair of abstract principles:

Reasons: The fact that p is a reason for A to φ just in case A has a collection of psychological states, C, such that the disposition to be moved to φ by C-and-the-belief-that-p is a good disposition of practical thought, and C contains no false beliefs.

The Virtue Theory: Being good as a disposition of practical thought is being a disposition of practical thought that is good as a trait of character.

When we ask how we should live or what we should do, our questions are equivalent to ones about the balance of reasons, and these in turn to questions about dispositions of practical thought. To assess such dispositions *as* dispositions of practical thought is not to appeal to standards that derive from the nature of the thought that they deploy, as in ethical rationalism, but simply to ask whether they are good as traits of character. We have no grip on what it is to think well about how to live and how to act, apart from our grip on what it is for a person to be good.

It is important to stress, once again, that these claims are basically symmetric. I am not saying that the concept of good character has what Watson calls "*explanatory primacy*" (1990: 451). The metaphysical connection between reasons and virtues runs in both directions. Insofar as we find asymmetry here, it lies in two things.[1] First, the idea of good character is not restricted in application to dispositions of practical thought. It can also be applied, for instance, to emotional dispositions

---

[1] The following remarks depend on the arguments of Part Two, section 1: "Character and Practical Thought."

that have no immediate bearing on the motivation of action, intention, or desire. Second, the idea of a good disposition of practical thought is not restricted to dispositions of the kind that figure in *Reasons*. There are, for instance, the dispositions of practical thought that constitute our sensitivity to the facts: how we *form* the beliefs that bear on the motivation of action, intention, and desire. And there are dispositions that bear on the options we consider. So the picture is one of concentric circles. In the narrowest circle, we can speak equivalently of reasons and of dispositions to be moved by collections of psychological states that include the relevant beliefs. In a broader circle, we can speak of dispositions of practical thought as being good or bad, as such, in that they are good or bad as traits of character. And then we can speak of good character, in general, whether or not it bears on the content of practical thought.[2]

The crucial point is that these asymmetries of scope do not imply any further asymmetry. In particular, nothing follows about the *epistemic* priorities of practical reason and ethical virtue. It is not part of the virtue theory that our beliefs about what there is reason to do must always be derived from claims about good character that are antecedently justified, or that arguments cannot run the other way. This means that if we come to accept the virtue theory, having been originally sceptical, we can revise our beliefs in three ways. We can hold fixed our beliefs about reasons, and revise our beliefs about the virtues of character; we can do the opposite of that; or we can find some compromise between the two. The only firm condition is that we must achieve an equilibrium that is consistent with *Reasons* and the virtue theory.

So, for instance, it does not follow from the arguments so far, considered on their own, that *instrumentalism* about practical reason is false. In Part Two, I criticized the rationalist form of instrumentalism. But even if that fails, the instrumentalist can maintain his view, that the object of practical reason is the satisfaction of desire, without rejecting the virtue theory—*if* he is willing to insist that means-end efficiency is the only virtue of character. If the instrumentalist is seriously prepared to accept a picture of the virtuous person as merely efficient—to deny that justice, benevolence, and courage are virtues—he need not dispute any of the arguments I have given above. I take it that one task of Warren Quinn's paper, "Rationality and the Human Good," is to embarrass the proponent of such a view (1992). As he argues, means-end efficiency is indiffer-

---

[2] There are broader circles too: psychological dispositions, dispositions in general, and so on. It is implicit in the arguments of Part Two that some evaluative distinctions are possible here—for instance, between epistemic dispositions directed at belief and thus at truth, and the dispositions that constitute one's ethical character. Unfortunately, I cannot address these matters here.

ent to the shamefulness and even the pettiness of ends. It is hard to credit this as a picture of the good person, even if one is sceptical of common-sense conceptions of ethical virtue. If the instrumentalist is committed to a picture of the virtuous person on which she may be contemptible, petty, and indifferent to shame, that is as close to a *reductio* as we should hope to get.

There is a further question, whether means-end efficiency is not only not the whole of virtue, but even, unequivocally, part of it. Is the general disposition to want (what one takes to be) the means to one's ends, regardless of the content of those ends, a good trait of character? What about the case in which one's ends are bad?[3] It is at least arguable that the disposition to desire the means to wicked or petty or contemptible ends is *not* a good trait of character, so that, on the present account, instrumental reasoning is not unconditionally good. The peculiarity of this claim can be softened in two ways. First, in the context of *Reasons* and the virtue theory, it corresponds to the claim that there is no reason to take the means to vicious ends. That view may be controversial, but it is not especially strange. Second, the occasional defects of instrumental reasoning from desire are perfectly consistent with the fact that *reasons* transmit from ends to means: if there is good reason to adopt an end, there is good reason to take the means to its satisfaction. The claim being cast in doubt is that there is always reason to take the means to one's ends, whatever those ends may be.[4]

The questions I am raising here, about whether a given trait or disposition counts as good character, might be settled by a metaphysical theory of virtue. In recent years, attempts at such a metaphysics have tended to follow an Aristotelian and broadly naturalistic line. One finds accounts of this kind sketched in Thompson (1995)—following Anscombe (1958: 38, 41)—and more elaborately worked out by MacIntyre (1999), Hursthouse (1999, Part III), and Foot (2001). I am sympathetic to some of these ideas, but sceptical of others.[5] It is not easy to be sure in the absence

[3] These questions are addressed in Setiya (2005), where they are deployed in an argument against the instrumentalist. That argument is independent of the issues about ethical rationalism and the Difference Principle that have been central to this book.

[4] On the distinction between these versions of the "instrumental principle"—one beginning with ends as desires, the other with reasons for ends—see Broome (1997: 133–8).

[5] In particular, contemporary Aristotelians tend to make use of *teleological* or *functional* concepts, but to reject the relevance to their inquiry of work in the philosophy of biology. (See Foot 2001: 32 n.10, 40 n. 1.) It is hard to accept that there is an ambiguity here, between the sense of "function" that biologists or zoologists employ, and the sense that figures in the metaphysics of living things. There needs to be a meeting of minds between philosophers of science who are interested in biological teleology and moral philosophers who hope for a teleological approach to ethical virtue and the human good.

of any comparable development of the "sentimentalist" virtue ethics of Hutcheson and Hume. The sentimentalists of the eighteenth century have figured in recent philosophical debate primarily as non-cognitivists about moral judgement, not as the theorists of virtue they took themselves to be.[6] In any case, as I mentioned in the introduction to this book, my argument has been effectively neutral on the metaphysics of virtue, and I want to sustain that neutrality here.

Nevertheless, I remain quite sure that justice, courage, and benevolence are virtues of character. And even without a metaphysics of virtue, I think we can see that it is, in general, more rational to react to the virtue theory by revising one's beliefs about reasons, bringing them into line with one's beliefs about ethical virtue, than to go the other way. The relevant asymmetry is this: nothing I have said in this book suggests that our convictions about good character derive from a deceptive or misleading source; by contrast, insofar as we are prone to think in *rationalist* terms, our convictions about what there is reason to do depend on a mistake. When there is a conflict between two sets of beliefs, and we have reason to fear that one of them is supported or infected by error, it is the other set that ought to be preserved.

The question, then, is whether and to what extent our beliefs about reasons can be traced to a potentially tacit assumption of ethical rationalism. It is not easy to generalize about this, since it depends on the person whose beliefs are at stake. But given the arguments of Part Two, we can say at least three things. First, that the appeal of instrumentalism derives in part from the (bad) idea that practical thought must be fueled by desire. Second, that it is a mistake to assume, as many do, that conceptions of practical reason can only be recognitional or constructivist. And finally, that internalism about practical reason is itself a form of ethical rationalism. If these three claims are right, the rationalist doctrine is often at work where it may not initially seem to be, shaping our sense of the possible or plausible views. It is in the air that moral philosophers breathe. It follows that, confronted with the virtue theory, one probably should not revise one's beliefs about ethical virtue, but about what there is reason to do.

If you are like me, you will be left with a picture of the virtuous person as being just, benevolent, and brave—but also prudent, and efficient in the pursuit of her own ends (so long as they are not vicious in themselves). And you will conclude that the sorts of considerations to which these virtues make one sensitive provide us all with reasons to act. It is hard to

---

[6] Snare (1991) is a recent proponent of the non-cognitivist reading of Hume. Versions of non-cognitivism survive in Gibbard (1990) and the essays in Part II of Blackburn (1993).

[7] This mistake is made by Cullity and Gaut (1997: 4–5), by Korsgaard (1996: 34–7), and by Wedgwood (2003: 206–7), among others.

content of good character indefinite S/k
the virtues not defined each by
← list of dispositions.

735 - 5

be more definite about the content of good character, in part because, as I argued in Part Two, the virtues are not defined each by a list of dispositions. There are different ways of being honest or compassionate, prudent or brave, and different ways to balance these virtues against one another. In particular, even though justice and benevolence are virtues, I think one can be a good person without being a moral saint.

It is not my project here to work out the details of this, or to establish the merits of the traditional virtues of character. The principal consequence of the virtue theory does not depend on what the virtues are, but on the fact that they form the subject-matter for questions of practical reason. On the face of it, there are two kinds of moral sceptic, one who doubts or rejects our beliefs about moral virtue, the other who grants those beliefs, and then asks why they should matter to him. The first kind of sceptic is like Nietzsche, or Callicles in the *Gorgias*, throwing over common sense about what makes us good, and putting something radical in its place. Or he is like John Mackie: he denies that there is any such thing as an ethical fact. This kind of sceptic has seen his share of attention in recent years. But moral philosophers have been at least as much concerned with the sceptic of the second kind, one who grants that a virtuous person would be just and benevolent, in the ordinary sense, and then denies that there is reason for him to care. Why should he act as a *good* person would act, in the circumstance that he is in? If the virtue theory is true, this question makes no sense. The idea that the ethical "should" comes apart from ethical virtue depends on ethical rationalism, and so it depends on something false. Questions of practical reason are *equivalent* to ones about good character. The real threat is Nietzsche or Callicles, or John Mackie, not the "fool" of the *Leviathan* or Hume's "sensible knave." This is the final moral of the virtue theory: insofar as its task is to answer the second kind of sceptic, by giving him reasons to do what it is admittedly virtuous to do, moral philosophy rests on a mistake.

BIBLIOGRAPHY

Allison, H. 1986: Morality and freedom: Kant's reciprocity thesis, *Philosophical Review* (95): 393–425.

Altham, J. 1986: The legacy of emotivism, in L. MacDonald and C. Wright, eds., *Fact, Science and Morality*, Oxford: Basil Blackwell, 1986: 275–88.

Anscombe, G.E.M. 1958: Modern moral philosophy, in her *Ethics, Religion and Politics*, Oxford: Basil Blackwell, 1981: 26–42.

———. 1963: *Intention*; second edition. Oxford: Basil Blackwell.

———. 1983: The causation of action, in C. Ginet and S. Shoemaker, eds., *Knowledge and Mind*, Oxford: Oxford University Press, 1983: 174–90.

———. 1989: Practical inference, in R. Hursthouse, G. Lawrence and W. Quinn, eds., *Virtues and Reasons*, Oxford: Oxford University Press, 1995: 1–34.

Arpaly, N. 2003: *Unprincipled Virtue*. Oxford: Oxford University Press.

Audi, R. 1986: Acting for reasons, in A. Mele, ed., *The Philosophy of Action*, Oxford: Oxford University Press, 1997: 75–105.

Blackburn, S. 1993: *Essays in Quasi-Realism*. Oxford: Oxford University Press.

Blum, L. 1991: Moral perception and particularity, *Ethics* (101): 701–25.

Bond, E. J. 1983: *Reason and Value*. Cambridge: Cambridge University Press.

Bratman, M. 1981: Intention and means-end reasoning, *Philosophical Review* (90): 252–65.

———. 1984: Two faces of intention, *Philosophical Review* (93): 375–405.

———. 1987: *Intention, Plans and Practical Reason*. Cambridge, MA: Harvard University Press.

———. 1991: Cognitivism about practical reason, in his *Faces of Intention*, Cambridge: Cambridge University Press, 1999: 250–64.

Brink, D. 1992: A puzzle about the rational authority of morality, *Philosophical Perspectives* (6): 1–26.

Broome, J. 1997: Reason and motivation, *Proceedings of the Aristotelian Society, Supplementary Volume* (71): 131–46.

———. 1999: Normative requirements, in J. Dancy, ed., *Normativity*, Oxford: Basil Blackwell, 2000: 78–99.

———. 2001: Normative practical reasoning, *Proceedings of the Aristotelian Society, Supplementary Volume* (75): 175–93.

Burnyeat, M. 1980: Aristotle on learning to be good, in A. Rorty, ed., *Essays on Aristotle's Ethics*, Berkeley, CA: University of California Press, 1980: 69–92.

Chang, R., ed. 1997: *Incommensurability, Incomparability and Practical Reason*. Cambridge, MA: Harvard University Press.

Cherniak, C. 1986: *Minimal Rationality*. Cambridge, MA: MIT Press.

Cooper, J. M., ed. 1997: *Plato: Complete Works*. Indianapolis, IN: Hackett Publishing.

Cullity, G. and Gaut, B., eds. 1997: *Ethics and Practical Reason*. Oxford: Oxford University Press.

Dancy, J. 2000: *Practical Reality*. Oxford: Oxford University Press.

Darwall, S. 1983: *Impartial Reason*. Ithaca, NY: Cornell University Press.

Davidson, D. 1963: Actions, reasons, and causes, in his 1980: 3–19.

———. 1970a: How is weakness of the will possible? In his 1980: 21–42.

———. 1970b: Mental events, in his 1980: 207–25.

———. 1971: Agency, in his 1980: 43–61.

———. 1973: Freedom to act, in his 1980: 63–81.

———. 1974: Psychology as philosophy, in his 1980: 229–39.

———. 1978: Intending, in his 1980: 83–102.

———. 1980: *Essays on Actions and Events*. Oxford: Oxford University Press.

———. 1987: Problems in the explanation of action, in his *Problems of Rationality*, Oxford: Oxford University Press, 2004: 101–16.

Doris, J. 1998: Persons, situations and virtue ethics, *Noûs* (32): 504–30.

Dorr, C. 2004: Non-symmetric relations, in D. Zimmerman, ed., *Oxford Studies in Metaphysics*, Oxford: Oxford University Press, 2004: 155–92.

Dostoevsky, F. 1869: *The Idiot*, D. Magarshack, trans., Harmondsworth: Penguin, 1955.

Dreier, J. 1996: Rational preference: decision theory as a theory of practical rationality, *Theory and Decision* (40): 249–76.

———. 1997: Humean doubts about the practical justification of morality, in Cullity and Gaut, eds., 1997: 81–100.

Falvey, K. 2000: Knowledge in intention, *Philosophical Studies* (99): 21–44.

Fine, K. 1994: Essence and modality, *Philosophical Perspectives* (8): 1–16.

Foot, P. 1958-9: Moral beliefs, in her 1978: 110–31.

———. 1961: Goodness and choice, in her 1978: 132–47.

———. ed. 1967: *Theories of Ethics*. Oxford: Oxford University Press.

———. 1972: Morality as a system of hypothetical imperatives, in her 1978: 157–73.

———. 1978: *Virtues and Vices*. Oxford: Basil Blackwell.

———. 1985: Utilitarianism and the virtues, *Mind* (94): 196–209.

———. 2001: *Natural Goodness*. Oxford: Oxford University Press.

Frankfurt, H. 1971: Freedom of the will and the concept of a person, in his 1988: 11–25.

———. 1978: The problem of action, in his 1988: 69–79.

———. 1988: *The Importance of What We Care About*. Cambridge: Cambridge University Press.

———. 1992: On the usefulness of final ends, in his *Necessity, Volition, and Love*, Cambridge: Cambridge University Press, 1999: 82–94.

Freud, S. 1901: *The Psychopathology of Everyday Life*, A. Tyson, transl., New York, NY: Norton, 1989.

Gauthier, D. 1986: *Morals by Agreement*. Oxford: Oxford University Press.

Geach, P. 1956: Good and evil, in Foot, ed., 1967: 64–73.

Gewirth, A. 1978: *Reason and Morality*. Chicago, IL: University of Chicago Press.

Gibbard, A. 1990: *Wise Choices, Apt Feelings*. Cambridge, MA: Harvard University Press.

———. 1999: Morality as consistency in living: Korsgaard's Kantian lectures, *Ethics* (109): 140–64.

Ginet, C. 1989: Reasons explanation of action: an incompatibilist account, *Philosophical Perspectives* (3): 17–46.

Hamlyn, D. W. 1968: *Aristotle: De Anima, Books II and III*. Oxford: Oxford University Press.

Hampshire, S. and Hart, H.L.A. 1958: Decision, intention and certainty, *Mind* (67): 1–12.

Hampshire, S. 1959: *Thought and Action*. Notre Dame, IN: University of Notre Dame Press.

Hampton, J. 1995: Does Hume have an instrumental conception of practical reason? *Hume Studies* (21): 57–74.

———. 1998: *The Authority of Reason*. Cambridge: Cambridge University Press.

Hare, R. M. 1957: Geach: good and evil, in Foot, ed., 1967: 74–82.

Harman, G. 1976: Practical reasoning, in A. Mele, ed., *The Philosophy of Action*, Oxford: Oxford University Press, 1997: 149–77.

———. 1986: *Change in View*. Cambridge, MA: MIT Press.

———. 1995: Rationality, in his *Reasoning, Meaning and Mind*, Oxford: Clarendon Press, 1999: 9–45.

———. 1999: Moral philosophy meets social psychology: virtue ethics and the fundamental attribution error, *Proceedings of the Aristotelian Society* (99): 315–31.

Hanser, M. 1998: Intention and teleology, *Mind* (107): 381–401.

———. 2000: Intention and accident, *Philosophical Studies* (98): 17–36.

Heinaman, R., ed. 1995: *Aristotle and Moral Realism*. London: UCL Press.

Hobart, R. E. 1934: Free will as involving determinism and inconceivable without it, *Mind* (43): 1–27.

Hobbes, T. 1650: *Leviathan*, E. Curley, ed., Indianapolis, IN: Hackett Publishing, 1994.

Holton, R. 1999: Intention and weakness of will, *Journal of Philosophy* (96): 241–62.

Hooker, B. 1987: Williams' argument against external reasons, *Analysis* (47): 42–4.

Hooker, B. and Little, M., eds. 2000: *Moral Particularism*. Oxford: Oxford University Press.

Hornsby, J. 1980: *Actions*. London: Routledge and Kegan Paul.

Hume, D. 1739–40: *A Treatise of Human Nature*, D. F. Norton and M. J. Norton, eds., Oxford: Oxford University Press, 2000.

———. 1751: *An Enquiry Concerning the Principles of Morals*, T. L. Beauchamp, ed., Oxford: Oxford University Press, 1998.

Hurka, T. 2001: *Virtue, Vice and Value*. Oxford: Oxford University Press.

Hursthouse, R. 1991: Arational actions, *Journal of Philosophy* (88): 57–68.

———. 1995: The virtuous agent's reasons: a reply to Bernard Williams, in Heinaman, ed., 1995: 24–34.

———. 1999: *On Virtue Ethics*. Oxford: Oxford University Press.

Hutcheson, F. 1726: *An Inquiry into the Original of Our Ideas of Beauty and Virtue*, W. Leidhold, ed., Indianapolis, IN: Liberty Fund, 2004.

Hutcheson, F. 1728: *An Essay on the Nature and Conduct of the Passions and Affection, with Illustrations on the Moral Sense*, A. Garrett, ed., Indianapolis, IN: Liberty Fund, 2002.

Hyman, J. 1999: How knowledge works, *Philosophical Quarterly* (49): 433–51.

Irwin, T., transl. 1999: Aristotle, *Nicomachean Ethics*; second edition. Indianapolis, IN: Hackett Publishing.

James, H. 1881: *The Portrait of a Lady*, G. Moore, ed., Harmondsworth: Penguin, 1986.

Johnston, M. 2001: The authority of affect, *Philosophy and Phenomenological Research* (63): 181–214.

Jones, O. R. 1983: Trying, *Mind* (92): 368–85.

Juarrero, A. 1999: *Dynamics in Action*. Cambridge, MA: MIT Press.

Kant, I. 1785: *Groundwork of the Metaphysics of Morals*, M. Gregor, transl., Cambridge: Cambridge University Press, 1998.

———. 1788: *Critique of Practical Reason*, M. Gregor, transl., Cambridge: Cambridge University Press, 1997.

Kavka, G. 1983: The toxin puzzle, *Analysis* (43): 33–6.

Kolnai, A. 1977: Deliberation is of ends, in his *Ethics, Value and Reality*, London: Athlone Press, 1977: 44–62.

Korsgaard, C. 1986: Skepticism about practical reason, in her *Creating the Kingdom of Ends*, Cambridge: Cambridge University Press, 1996: 311–34.

———. 1996: *The Sources of Normativity*. Cambridge: Cambridge University Press.

———. 1997: The normativity of instrumental reason, in Cullity and Gaut, eds., 1997: 215–54.

———. 1999: *The Myth of Egoism*. Lawrence, KA: Lindley Lecture, Department of Philosophy, University of Kansas.

MacIntyre, A. 1999: *Dependent Rational Animals*. Chicago, IL: Open Court.

Mackie, J. L. 1977: *Ethics: Inventing Right and Wrong*. Harmondsworth: Penguin.

McDowell, J. 1978: Are moral requirements hypothetical imperatives? In his 1998: 77–94.

———. 1979: Virtue and reason, in his 1998: 50–73.

———. 1980: The role of *eudaimonia* in Aristotle's ethics, in his 1998: 3–22.

———. 1985: Functionalism and anomalous monism, in his 1998: 325–40.

———. 1995a: Might there be external reasons? In his 1998: 95–111.

———. 1995b: Two sorts of naturalism, in his 1998: 167–97.

———. 1998: *Mind, Value and Reality*. Cambridge, MA: Harvard University Press.

Mele, A. 1987: *Irrationality*. Oxford: Oxford University Press.

———. 1992: *Springs of Action*. Oxford: Oxford University Press.

Mellor, D. H. 1977–8: Conscious belief, *Proceedings of the Aristotelian Society* (78): 87–101.

———. 1993: How to believe a conditional, *Journal of Philosophy* (90): 233–48.

Millgram, E. 1995: Was Hume a Humean? *Hume Studies* (21): 75–93.

———. 1996: Williams' argument against external reasons, *Noûs* (30): 197–220.

Milligan, D. E. 1974: Reasons as explanations, *Mind* (83): 180–93.

Murdoch, I. 1970: *The Sovereignty of Good*. London: Routledge and Kegan Paul.

Nagel, T. 1970: *The Possibility of Altruism*. Princeton, NJ: Princeton University Press.

Nussbaum, M. 1988: Non-relative virtues: an Aristotelian approach, *Midwest Studies in Philosophy* (13): 32–53.

O'Neill, O. 1985: Consistency in action, in N. Potter and M. Timmons, eds., *Universality and Morality*, Dordrecht, Holland: D. Reidel Publishing Company, 1985: 158–86.

O'Shaughnessy, B. 1973: Trying (as the Mental "Pineal Gland"), *Journal of Philosophy* (70): 365–86.

Parfit, D. 1984: *Reasons and Persons*. Oxford: Oxford University Press.

——. 1997: Reasons and motivation, *Proceedings of the Aristotelian Society, Supplementary Volume* (71): 99–130.

Pettit, P. and Price, H. 1989: Bare functional desire, *Analysis* (49): 162–69.

Pettit, P. and Smith, M. 1990: Backgrounding desire, *Philosophical Review* (99): 565–92.

Pieper, J. 1966: *The Four Cardinal Virtues*. Notre Dame, IN: University of Notre Dame Press.

Pigden, C. 1990: Geach on 'good', *Philosophical Quarterly* (40): 129–54.

Piller, C. 1996: Critical notice: Michael Smith, *The Moral Problem*, *Australasian Journal of Philosophy* (74): 347–67.

Prichard, H. 1912: Does moral philosophy rest on a mistake? In his *Moral Writings*, Oxford: Clarendon Press, 2002: 7–20.

Pryor, J. 2000: The skeptic and the dogmatist, *Noûs* (34): 517–49.

Quinn, W. 1992: Rationality and the human good, in his *Morality and Action*, Cambridge: Cambridge University Press, 1993: 210–27.

——. 1993: Putting rationality in its place, in his *Morality and Action*, Cambridge: Cambridge University Press, 1993: 228–55.

Railton, P. 1997: On the hypothetical and non-hypothetical in reasoning about belief and action, in Cullity and Gaut, eds., 1997: 53–80.

Rawls, J. 1971: *A Theory of Justice*. Cambridge, MA: Harvard University Press.

——. 1980: Kantian constructivism in moral theory, in his *Collected Papers*, S. Freeman, ed., Cambridge, MA: Harvard University Press, 1999: 303–58.

Raz. J. 1997: When we are ourselves: the active and the passive, in his *Engaging Reason*, Oxford: Oxford University Press, 1999: 5–21.

——. 1999: Agency, reason and the good, in his *Engaging Reason*, Oxford: Oxford University Press, 1999: 22–45.

Richardson, H. 1994: *Practical Reasoning About Final Ends*. Cambridge: Cambridge University Press.

Ross, L. and Nisbet, R. E. 1991: *The Person and the Situation: Perspectives of Social Psychology*. New York, NY: McGraw-Hill.

Scanlon, T. M. 1998: *What We Owe to Each Other*. Cambridge, MA: Harvard University Press.

Schmidtz, D. 1994: Choosing ends, *Ethics* (104): 226–51.

Schueler, G. F. 1995: *Desire: Its Role in Practical Reason and the Explanation of Action*. Cambridge, MA: MIT Press.

Searle, J. 1983: *Intentionality*. Cambridge: Cambridge University Press.

———. 2001: *Rationality in Action*. Cambridge, MA: MIT Press.

Segvic, H. 2000: No one errs willingly: the meaning of Socratic intellectualism, *Oxford Studies in Ancient Philosophy* (19): 1–45.

Setiya, K. 2004a: Against internalism, *Noûs* (38): 266–98.

———. 2004b: Explaining action, *Philosophical Review* (112): 339–93.

———. 2004c: Hume on practical reason, *Philosophical Perspectives* (18): 365–89.

———. 2005: Is efficiency a vice? *American Philosophical Quarterly* (42): 333–39.

Shope, R. 1978: The conditional fallacy in contemporary philosophy, *Journal of Philosophy* (75): 397–413.

Slote, M. 1992: *From Morality to Virtue*. Oxford: Oxford University Press.

Smith, M. 1987: The Humean theory of motivation, *Mind* (96): 36–61.

———. 1994: *The Moral Problem*. Cambridge: Cambridge University Press.

———. 1995: Internal reasons, *Philosophy and Phenomenological Research* (55): 109–31.

———. 1998: The possibility of philosophy of action, in his *Ethics and the A Priori*, Cambridge: Cambridge University Press, 2004: 155–77.

Snare, F. 1991: *Morals, Motivation and Convention: Hume's Influential Doctrines*. Cambridge: Cambridge University Press.

Sreenivasan, G. 2002: Errors about errors: virtue theory and trait attribution, *Mind* (111): 47–68.

Stalnaker, R. 1984: *Inquiry*. Cambridge, MA: MIT Press.

Stampe, D. 1987: The authority of desire, *Philosophical Review* (96): 335–81.

Stocker, M. 1979: Desiring the bad, *Journal of Philosophy* (76): 738–53.

Stroud, S. and Tappolet, C., eds. 2003: *Weakness of Will and Practical Irrationality*. Oxford: Oxford University Press.

Szabó, Z. G. 2001: Adjectives in context, in R. Harnish and I. Kenesi, eds., *Perspectives on Semantics, Pragmatics and Discourse*, Amsterdam: John Benjamins, 2001: 119–46.

Tenenbaum, S. 2003: *Accidie*, evaluation, and motivation, in Stroud and Tappolet, eds., 2003: 147–71.

Thompson, M. 1995: The representation of life, in R. Hursthouse, G. Lawrence and W. Quinn, eds., *Virtues and Reasons*, Oxford: Oxford University Press, 1995: 247–96.

———. Forthcoming: Naïve action theory, in his *Life and Action*, Cambridge, MA: Harvard University Press.

Thomson, J. J. 1992: On some ways in which a thing can be good, *Social Philosophy and Policy* (9:2): 96–117.

Velleman, J. D. 1989: *Practical Reflection*. Princeton, NJ: Princeton University Press.

———. 1992a: The guise of the good, in his 2000b: 99–122.

———. 1992b: What happens when someone acts? In his 2000b: 123–43.

———. 1996: The possibility of practical reason, in his 2000b: 170–99.

———. 1997: Deciding how to decide, in his 2000b: 221–43.

Velleman, J. D. 2000a: On the aim of belief, in his 2000b: 244–81.

———. 2000b: *The Possibility of Practical Reason*. Oxford: Oxford University Press.

———. 2000c: From self psychology to moral philosophy, *Philosophical Perspectives* (14): 349-377.

Walker, A. F. 1989: The problem of weakness of will, *Noûs* (23): 653–76.

Wallace, R. J. 1991: Virtue, reason and principle, *Canadian Journal of Philosophy* (21): 469–95.

———. 1999: Three conceptions of rational agency, *Ethical Theory and Moral Practice* (2): 217–42.

Watson, G. 1975: Free agency, *Journal of Philosophy* (72): 205–20.

———. 1977: Skepticism about weakness of will, *Philosophical Review* (86): 316–39.

———. 1984: Virtues in excess, *Philosophical Studies* (46): 57–74.

———. 1990: On the primacy of character, in O. Flanagan and A. Rorty, eds., *Identity, Character and Morality*, Cambridge, MA: MIT Press, 1990: 449–69.

———. 2003: The work of the will, in Stroud and Tappolet, eds., 2003: 172–200.

Wedgwood, R. 1998: The fundamental principle of practical reasoning, *International Journal of Philosophical Studies* (6): 189–209.

———. 2002: The aim of belief, *Philosophical Perspectives* (16): 267–97.

———. 2003: Choosing rationally and choosing correctly, in Stroud and Tappolet, eds., 2003: 201–29.

White, S. 1990: Rationality, responsibility and pathological indifference, in O. Flanagan and A. Rorty, eds., *Identity, Character and Morality*, Cambridge, MA: MIT Press, 1990: 401–26.

Wiggins, D. 1975/6: Deliberation and practical reason, in his *Needs, Values, Truth*; third edition, Oxford: Oxford University Press, 1998: 215–38.

Williams, B. 1976: Persons, character and morality, in his 1981: 1–19.

———. 1980: Internal and external reasons, in his 1981: 101–13.

———. 1981: *Moral Luck*. Cambridge: Cambridge University Press.

———. 1985: *Ethics and the Limits of Philosophy*. Cambridge, MA: Harvard University Press.

———. 1989: Internal reasons and the obscurity of blame, in his *Making Sense of Humanity*, Cambridge: Cambridge University Press, 1995: 35–45.

———. 1995a: Replies, in J. Altham and R. Harrison, eds., *World, Mind and Ethics: Essays on the Ethical Philosophy of Bernard Williams*, Cambridge: Cambridge University Press, 1995: 185–224.

———. 1995b: Acting as the virtuous person acts, in Heinaman, ed., 1995: 13–23.

Wilson, G. 1989: *The Intentionality of Human Action*. Stanford, CA: Stanford University Press.

Wittgenstein, L. 1953: *Philosophical Investigations*, G.E.M. Anscombe, transl., Oxford: Basil Blackwell.

Index